Dear Body

Dear Body

How to fall in love with your body

and heal the world around you

Karen Chenery

Copyright © 2022 Karen Chenery
All rights reserved
ISBN-13: 9798458902038

Table of Contents

Introduction
13

A Realisation.
15

You Are Too Priceless To Measure.
20

A Letter To My Body.
29

Your Body Is Not A Project, It Is Your Companion On Your Life Journey.
35

The Argument For 'Changing Sh*t Up'.
43

Can You Really Breathe In Forever?
55

It Turns Out You Can Change The World
60

Treat Others How You Wish To Be Treated.
71

Pray, Love… Eat. The Importance Of Attaching Love And Positivity To The Food We Eat.
83

"UgUg" We Are More Cave-Person Than We Realise.
88

Addicted To Food/Fear/Shame/love
100

I Hear Ya' Tummy!
107

Good Vibrations. How To Test Your Resonance With Food.
114

Craving Freedom From Cravings.
124

The Emotional Link To Food. "Be A Good Girl, Have One More Mouthful!"
134

Forest Gump Didn't Run To Lose Weight.
146

The Gift Of Another Day.
154

Knowing Me, Knowing You. How Our Relationship With Our Own Body And Self Is Pivotal To All Our Other Relationships.
159

Fight, Flight, Feast Or Famine.
173

A Letter From Me To You.
183

Appendices
187

Preface

My sister started proof reading this book for me and then went a little quiet on the subject, I asked her for feedback and honest as ever, she said 'it feels a little angry, like you are cross with the reader'. She quoted a few passages and I totally saw what she meant, I said I would rewrite whole chapters and edit further.

In the meantime I pondered on how a book written out of love and with the aim of helping, could end up with quite a few chapters seeming like I was angry and cross. After a few days I realised two things; firstly, I wasn't cross with whoever would one day read this book, instead I was still angry with myself, for being so self abusive for all those years and this anger meant I was still allowing my perfectionism to have a say. It was saying, 'these days you are being very good at loving your body and having a healthy relationship with food. You didn't in

Dear Body

the past, you were *failing* at loving your body.' Trying to fit into a predetermined version of 'perfect' had always been the problem... and there it was, perfectionism still fuelling my emotions. I am a recovering perfectionist, I now know I need to be self aware and keep checking in. 'Am I comparing my body to others? Am I attaching negative thoughts to my image or food? Am I angry I've not 'succeeded' in being compassionate to myself?' I took a deep breath and continued to edit, but I decided to leave a bit of angry in the book, which leads me to my second point.

I am so passionate about the power and importance of how we talk about and treat our own bodies. I believe its impact is so pivotal, so life changing, that I had typed my way to a frenzy of urgent anger – *Please listen! Please understand you are worthy!* – This book is a passionate plea, that we don't need to self abuse, compare or torture our bodies.

Preface

My niece gets the wheel of her tricycle stuck, she tries and tries to release it, to no avail. She gets frustrated, then she gets angry. I used to think, 'she will learn to deal calmly in time.' And she will, for the little things, but I hope she will always keep her determination and passionate belief, that the wheel of her tricycle should not be stuck, because she has places to go and things to do.

Social structures, commercial fashion, beauty and media interests have been wedging the wheel of our tricycle for far too many years. For so long in fact that we have internalised those toxic beliefs. No wonder, when we realise the wheel can be unstuck, that we can believe and live differently, we start to shove and pull at the tricycle, we wail and scream at the stuck wheel, we cry at the injustice. We get angry! My glimmers of anger are me speeding along, all three wheels spinning on my metaphorical tricycle, but I'm still harbouring that anger and frustration from the memory of the stuck wheel. Anger with myself for not shifting it sooner and anger at

Dear Body

the structures and systems which wedged the tricycle wheel in the first place. I need to learn from my niece, as soon as the wheel of her tricycle is dislodged, she drops the associated emotions, no need for them anymore, she's busy speeding along grinning ear to ear.

This book is dedicated my niece, Meredith Quinn.

May you experience a world where people are allowed to feel all emotions are valid, where compassion and healing allows for emotions to be experienced in the present, so they don't reappear from the past. Where your determination and self worth, means you never accept a stuck tricycle wheel. Where acceptance and love of self is the only thing in fashion.

Preface

Trigger warning: this book is a tool to help heal, however due to its autobiographical nature, it contains aspects which some readers may find triggering around the topic of food, disordered eating and body dysmorphia.

This book does not aim to take the place of medical advice. Please seek professional help, I was helped by a qualified psychologist and my doctor. Please reach out to professionals and insist on getting the help you may need and which you deserve.

Introduction

Wonderful, incredible human, most beautiful soul… Stop hating yourself, stop shaming yourself, stop criticising your amazing body, and stop feeling guilty every time you eat or even think about food.

I know it's not easy, in some cases it's changing the habit of a lifetime, but this book aims to guide you through step by step, changing your relationship with yourself and your relationship with food. Looking at why it is so important that your relationship with food and with your own body is compassionate and loving. A negative view of yourself does not serve you or the wider good of those around you, it doesn't serve your health and wellbeing and it's frankly exhausting.

Dear Body

This book is written with love and with the goal of helping my fellow humans to move from pain, to self compassion and love. When you are content in your body, you are better placed to enjoy the good times and cope with the difficult times.

Chapter 1.

A Realisation.

I sat sobbing in my therapist's consulting room, broken, full of desperation at the fear of never being able to shrink my body into a size or shape that would be acceptable to me. I was exhausted by constantly trying to diet and trying to control everything. Running towards an ideal version of myself, whilst feeling like I might never get there.

My therapist looking suitably moved but unfazed, I garbled and sniffled through a few sentences which were going to prove to be my catalyst, my ultimate turning point, from which the only way was forward.

"I guess my relationship with food, my erratic exercising, my fad diets and eating disorders, my inability to love my body or spend even an hour, never mind a day, not thinking about losing weight or trying not to eat, is underpinned by my ultimate fear, if I am not quite the perfect finished article of myself that I am proud of, then if I am rejected or fail at something, I have an excuse. It's my body, my flawed not good enough body. If a boyfriend dumps me then it is because I ate that pain au chocolat last week, which made me gain a pound, so he found me repulsive. Also, If I give up my battle with my body what if the very next diet or vomit session works and I skip through a meadow finally able to love myself."

My therapist's sage response was, "What if you do put yourself out there? Would that be so bad?"

A Realisation

Cue a huge wail and uncontrollable sobbing. "Because I will be rejected by others, what if I'm not loved? What if I'm not good enough?"

"Well," said my therapist, I think now poised to see if her arrow of truth had paid off or was about to be something she wrote about under the title 'Unsuccessful.' "You have a choice," she continued, "drop your battle and risk what the outcome will be or carry on as you are. Either way there is a perceived risk, but there is a possibility that by dropping your battle with yourself and food, you find the happiness you deserve." In that moment I was willing to surrender in the battle against my body. I was exhausted and I wanted to live, more than that, I wanted to feel joy and self compassion.

I drove away from my appointment and headed towards my first task in my very new world of self acceptance… food shopping. The plan was to walk into M&S food at the local retail park and for the first time in my adult life, give myself permission to buy and then eat anything and importantly, everything I wanted.

I had spent years either hungry or stuffed with guilt, now I was heading towards the task of satisfying my hunger, whilst leaving out the side serving of guilt and shame.

As I walked through the doors and into the cool blast of air, I felt giddy with freedom! Anything! Anything! I can eat anything! I slowly walked the aisles taking in the colours, the options, the smells. I stopped and realised I felt something I hadn't felt in as long as I could remember. I have since named that feeling 'Zen Tummy.' There's an explanation of Zen Tummy waiting for you in a later chapter.

The first food shop following my breakthrough therapy session, not only changed my life, it gave birth to a theory, which I have since explored, researched, documented and lived. The theory has grown with me on

A Realisation

my recovery journey. I completed a psychology degree, embarked on a spiritual journey, became a Reiki Master, completed my Yoga Teacher Training and devoured books and information, which has helped me understand and develop this theory.

Chapter Two.

You Are Too Priceless To Measure.

Please throw your scales away. Go now to wherever you keep them in the house and rid your life of them. They are not weighing you, they are controlling you, they are a happiness barometer, a determiner of self acceptance, silently waiting for you to step on them so they can dictate in their luminous red numbers or flickering indecisive way, if you are allowed to hold your head up high today, if you are allowed to wear a summer dress today, or whether you are allowed to start chatting to that cute person on the bus today. Please do not let a little box that lingers on the floor determine your life path and decisions. Even if for now they only get as far as your car or the garden shed, evict them from your daily routine. I lovingly insist.

Now they are gone and you have had the faith and trust to do that, I will explain both from a psychological and biological perspective, but also from a spiritual perspective why scales do not help you in any way. Unless you were using them to weigh your luggage before your holiday, in which case, (pardon the pun) you can get much more accurate luggage scales. I would like to point out at this stage that psychological, biological and spiritual (read 'consciousness' if you don't like to say 'spiritual') are all inextricably linked, so will always have crossovers but for simplicity I have segregated them in explanation.

The psychological reasons not to use scales are firstly, you are way too long in the tooth to have a 'naughty step' and secondly, the scales will not ever reach a point where you are happy with what they say. Don't get me wrong, if your goal is to have the number '10' or the number '60' on your scales, you may reach that goal on perhaps a Tuesday, it will be a lovely day, a warm summer's breeze with not a cloud in the sky. Having stripped every scrap of clothing from your body and with one eye closed, you gingerly step on. The scale reads the exact number you have been hoping for, the holy grail, the number that means you have succeeded. But what if that day never comes, or it comes and then it goes again, what if they never read the magic worthy number you have given yourself... What then?

And beautiful soul, I do not ask that question lightly. As you have read, I spent a good chunk of my life, believing that unless my scales had certain numbers on them, I didn't want to live. As I write this, almost in a trance, so many years in recovery, tears still fall down my cheeks. I realise how terribly sad it is that any of us live even one day letting our happiness and self worth be dictated by the extent to which our beautiful, incredible bodies have the force of gravity enacting on us. That is what "weight" is, usually so steeped in our social norms related to body image. The Oxford English dictionary definition of "weight" is 'A body's relative mass or the quantity of matter contained by it, giving rise to a downward force'. How has this become a measure of worth or social acceptance? Maybe if aliens came to earth they would think we are all trying to appease the gravity gods, trying to shrink and shape our bodies and mirror each other so we all look like we have been spat out of the end of a 'human making' machine, rather than through the birth canal or abdomen of our mothers.

Later we explore how thinking about what our bodies weigh, is steeped in social norms, the logic of which we've rarely questioned. But what about the logic surrounding what our weight actually indicates for our biology? Last time I worked out my BMI it was very high, the reason being, I have very dense heavy bones. I can almost hear you all rolling around with laughter! 'She went to the effort of writing a whole book and it turns out she just thinks she has heavy bones!' Well yes I do.

Dear Body

Another person may have different weight and sized bones and body tissues, it turns out that what we are weighing and calculating, via scales, flesh pinching devices and various formulae is showing us precisely one thing… f*ck all!

Yes that was meant to shock, because I too needed that shock to wake myself up from the body measuring illusion. A physical, body jolting, mind melting realisation that someone might have a heavy thumb joint or a particularly light set of kidneys, or skinny feet or one thigh bigger than the other, or one eyelid saggier than the other or big nipples, or big ears or scar tissue, or life saving internal devices, or metal plates holding bones together, a uterus full of blood ready for conception or a stomach full of dinner, or maybe more circulating platelets in our blood, more air sacs in our lungs. And a widely accepted societal norm is to weigh ourselves.

So, I know from all the calculations I did in my early twenties that for the size of my frame, my bones are heavy, I don't know why and I don't care why, it's just me. So even when I looked like a skeleton, I believed the scales never quite said the right number. And even when everyone said 'aren't you so thin', I still felt I wasn't dodging the gods of gravity quite enough. I felt the scales were telling me I was taking up too much space on this planet.

I know some people are going to question my opinion that weight doesn't matter, after all even western medical professionals have a history of telling their patients to 'lose weight'. But weight actually shouldn't matter and yes, it's fine even if your body is so heavy you can't get out of bed. You are worthy, you are loved and you should accept yourself just as you are. Because once weight, ability and appearance don't factor in your decision, then self love and self acceptance can be achieved, then crucially, self abuse doesn't have anywhere to thrive and instead your health can thrive. Whether your weight and lack of self love limits your ability to get out of bed unassisted or whether it limits whether you feel comfortable walking into a room of colleagues, either way there is a false belief about yourself which is at the root of it all, it is the belief about yourself which is the key. No one ever said, I binge eat because I value myself, no one ever made themselves sick because they have so much self love. Nurture self love and the symptoms of lack of self worth and lack of self love, will naturally heal themselves. Your body will have no option but to come into line with the love and care you are showing it.

Biologically we are all unique, yes we have similarities but it is ludicrous for us to try and shoe horn ourselves into a supposed ideal. So, Beautiful soul, stop trying to measure your worth using gravity, I know that you are worthy and I am going to lead you on a journey so you can find a place of acceptance from which your self love can bloom. And here links the spiritual reason to get rid of your scales and the body measuring addiction. It does not honour the incredible soul that you are, it instead puts life on hold, it attaches clauses to living a full life "when I am… I will…" and "when I have… I can"

Take a pen and paper, ask yourself 'If I knew today that I have what I think is the 'perfect' body, what would I do that I have been putting off?' Writing down your answer will show you how much of your life you are waiting to be worthy of. When I asked myself this question years ago, my list included: dance sober, feel equal in my relationship, wear a crop top, be happy, stop hating myself, enjoy a beach holiday, start my own business, not worry what people thought of me, feel cool, feel like life can really begin.

Whatever is on your list, one thing I can tell you is whilst you are waiting to do all the things on your list, life is passing you by. Whilst you are waiting to live, you are existing. Existing feels stifled, boring, predictable, exhausting and potentially depressing. It feels like you are always waiting. Instead, let's start enjoying the journey, let's realise that life is one big journey, one big learning curve, we never get 'there' to that hallowed place where our bodies are perfect by toxic social norms, where we know everything and where there is nothing

Dear Body

else left to feel, or see, or love, or learn, or enjoy, because life is an ongoing experience. So today could be the first day that you will start to free yourself from waiting to live, the first day of not letting self hatred highjack your time, the first day you will say 'I love my body'. So, follow me and we'll get there together, step by step.

Chapter Three.

A Letter To My Body.

I am going to share with you a letter I wrote to myself as part of my recovery, it was hand written on lined A4 paper many years ago and then folded and tucked into a keepsake box. It's moved house with me and I have shared it with my therapist and my mum, but other than that it has just remained as a reminder of my humble apology to my body, my apology to myself and importantly of my pledge to myself going forward.

"Hello body. I feel a letter to you is well overdue, seeing as we've been together now for over 27 years.

Dear Body

I owe you a massive thank you, as together we have always been free from any serious illness. I feel at this stage in life though, I owe you a massive apology 'body'.

Unfortunately it's a bit like the apology an addict gives their loved ones… heartfelt, but flawed and not necessarily a watertight agreement for the future. In other words 'body' I can see the error in my ways in dealing with you, however, I feel that changing my ways completely in the future is going to be an ongoing task, that I may occasionally slip up on.

Anyway… here it is… I'm so very sorry 'body' from the bottom of our heart for… well, lots of things, but I'll start with… I'm sorry for hating you.

I'm sorry for trying not to feed you, even when you are screaming with hunger, I'm sorry for making you sick up food until your mouth and fingers had blisters. I'm sorry I have judged you so harshly. And never accepted you as good enough. If a parent had treated a child in that way it would be seen as horrific abuse. And so I am sorry for abusing you.

A Letter To My Body

I am sorry for the pain I put you through; the waxing, plucking, electrolysis, injections, blood tests, hangovers, horse riding accidents, broken bones.

I'm also sorry that I dragged you through the emotional pain with me. Even when I've been hurting, I've not stopped for a minute to realise you are hurting too; instead I've just made things worse by starving you, then being angry at you for demanding food.

I'm sorry I've tried to turn you into something you're not.

It's time I started to live by the phrase I wrote in my journal two years ago 'Don't strive to be someone else. Strive to be better at being yourself.'

But no, I shouted in my mind at you for having boobs too big… seriously, tummy too flabby, arms too hairy, hair too curly.

To illustrate how extreme I realise I've been with you body, I have even noticed that you dear fingers get labelled as fat if jewellery rings are too tight.

I don't know why I'm so mean, the easy answer could be media, horrendous gossip magazines etc. Maybe I saw my mum dislike her shape and so I learnt it from her, but to be honest body I can remember a time when I was very proud and protective of you. I never doubted you, you just were. We lived together in perfect harmony.

So what went wrong?

I think the doubt and rejection of you seeped in from outside influences. And the attention we got when I'd starved you for two weeks (for which I'm sorry) gave me such a kick, I felt accepted by everyone.

When I look back at times I think I've been fat I cringe as to what people thought of us, what they said about us.

I think any rejection in my life I've blamed on you 'body'. If you are too fat, too ugly to be loved and accepted then it means I cannot be to blame, the "me" inside is not who's rejected. So I am sorry body for deflecting this resentment onto you, for using you as my scapegoat.

One more apology and thank you is thank you for being so reliable, forgiving even when we are awake all through the night on a pressurised plane, with less oxygen than you need. You still work, every bit of you and for that I am eternally grateful.

Body I have always known in the times of calm and clarity that you are beautiful and amazing. We have done so much together and I now look forward to all the amazing things we are still yet to do.

I can't promise I'll be perfect, but I promise to try and treat you in the loving way I know you deserve.'

Step 1: Dear beloved one, take some quiet time to write a letter to your body. It may be different from mine, but it should be written as if your thoughts are separate from your physical body, so you can see your treatment of your body from an outsider perspective. Any activities in this book are to be done when you feel the time is right, only you can decide when you are ready to apologise to your body, when you are ready to apologise to yourself. But a word of advice, it will never feel completely comfortable, it is going to take a leap of faith, it is going to be cathartic and it is going to mark the beginning of a new life. But it is potentially going to be a

Dear Body

very emotional experience. Reach out for help at any time and only write this letter to your body, when you feel ready to take the step.

Chapter Four.

Your Body Is Not A Project, It Is Your Companion On Your Life Journey.

"The privilege of a lifetime, is being who you are,"
Joseph Campbell

The way we criticise our bodies, compare them and abuse them, ultimately has a root cause in how we relate to ourselves. Without delving too deeply into the cliché about being comfortable in our own skin, it is useful to notice that many of us don't even feel our skin is our own, don't even take responsibility for the bodies we inhabit and can't bring ourselves to live with and experience life through our bodies. We are going to address that in this next step. But first, a little about gratitude.

Every moment we are thankful, makes us healthier and gratitude is a choice, even in the darkest moments we have a choice to be grateful, a choice to be free in our minds. As Nelson Mandela, Terry Waite and many others can testify, being physically imprisoned does not have to mean you are imprisoned in your mind. We have such miraculous minds, which create whole worlds and scenarios without us even having to leave the comfort of our sofa. The power and the creativity that resides in your mind is awesome.

Gratitude, the thought and feeling of gratitude in our minds and bodies, changes our neural pathways, gratitude literally changes our mind. If we view our body as a prison, as a project, then in turn we create a prison for our creativity and for the voice inside. As Deepak Chopra says, "Gratitude cannot be prescribed, it is simply a choice." From gratitude we can choose compassion and freedom. If we come from hate and lack, we confine ourselves, our bodies, our creativity and our ability to help others. We live in lack, so our ability to live and to give, is lacking.

We can choose to be grateful in any scenario. We can choose to be free, we can choose to view our bodies with gratitude and compassion, we can choose to rewire our minds to love and appreciate our bodies. This will not only revolutionise your experience of being alive, I truly believe that loving and accepting your body and treating it with compassion will act as an immunisation against toxic societal programming, it will heal the divisive and harmful media rhetoric peddled by many outlets, it will enable you to walk in grace, to be at peace with your body and to be at peace with yourself.

Imagine that feeling you get when you really feel at one with someone, whether its a colleague, a friend, a lover, that feeling that anything is possible with this person, the creativity, the mountains that can be moved together. Now imagine you can create that feeling for yourself, even in solitude, that resonance that you are safe, you are worthy, you are loved. Yes we must always dig deep to learn and to grow, to develop as humans and as members of our community here on planet earth, but we should never doubt the intrinsic and unique worth of our soul and of each and every soul and their respective journeys. That miraculous soul, that learning, growing beautiful soul, needs a loving, sanctuary. Your body will only be a loving sanctuary if your mind aligns with the idea of nurturing and loving your body. When your mind can see the value of loving rather than hating your body, when your brain understands that your body is friend and not foe, then you have a companion, you aren't constantly living with an enemy, you aren't constantly watching your back and seeking out sanctuary in the company of others. When your body is no longer a project, when it is instead a valued and revered part of you, then your mind and body become a creative and powerful team together. Then you are no longer a prisoner in your own body, instead you have a life long companion, an integrated mind/body/soul unit which coexists to bring compassion and love to everyone around you.

Some of you may be thinking "I will be friends with my body when I have a six pack or when that random hair stops growing out of my nipple." But suspend any doubt for now, let's continue on our recovery, stride boldly on with our healing and to do that, I am going to have to reacquaint you with your physical body. This is so important because us humans have tried hating, loathing and rejecting our body and it has only caused us emotional pain, suffering and misery. So as Terry Waite wrote, *"At the end of the day, love and compassion will win."*

Step 2: Sitting relaxed in comfy clothes or naked, whatever feels right, take three deep breaths, stretch your arms up towards the sky, then bring your palms together in line with your heart and then gently rub your palms together. Close your eyes at this point if it helps and then imagine a part of your body. Try not to second guess, just go with your initial thought or instinct. If one doesn't come to mind then I'll pick one for you, your forearm.

Your hands should be warmer now and as you stop rubbing them together you should feel they are slightly tingly and maybe fizzing. Now open your eyes and place a hand on the chosen body part, in my example, my forearm. Without judging, just notice. Is your arm warm or cool? Does it feel dry or clammy, hairy or hairless? Now gently and lovingly squeeze, can you feel the muscles, the layers of skin and flesh, the bones and tendons? If it's available to you then smile, feel the happiness from the smile fizzing through your hand and onto the body part you are touching and looking at.

To close this activity, try the 'palm to sole' technique. Place your right hand on the sole of your left foot and your left hand on the sole of your right foot.

How does that feel? To me it felt alien. I realised that other than to wash them in the bath I hadn't felt my feet probably since I was a child. I realised that there is a world where the me inside can connect with the body I am in, not in a sexual way, not in a critical way, but in a loving way. I felt a surge of strangeness and energy when I first did the 'palm to sole' foot ritual. My palms felt soft and spindly through my feet and the bottoms of my feet felt undulating and strong beneath my palms.

During this activity, make sure you smile and always guard against negative thoughts. Try and repeat this with a different body part and then touching your feet, each day if possible. In time, along with touch, you can also look, look at a very small area to start with, one that doesn't trigger your criticism. Maybe a knee or the little bit of your calf you think looks muscly, find one tiny square inch and really look. Imagine how many nerve endings, how many cells and how many capillaries serve that tiny area. Start to feel in awe of what an incredible

Dear Body

machine your body is. If you feel you want to, keep a journal of your journey reacquainting yourself with your own body. Each day pick another part of your body and imagine the cells and the mechanisms that make your body utterly amazing. Smile and send gratitude for the brilliance of your body into every part you focus on.

Chapter Five.

The Argument For 'Changing Sh*t Up'.

"Scientists tell us that 98% of our 60,000 thoughts are repeats from the day before"

I would like to start this dark, but hopefully funny chapter by letting you into my brain, no longer my life I hasten to add, this was me in my early 20's. But I think its helpful to share because, like a conservationist restoring a tattered masterpiece or a builder correcting subsidence in a building, one has to take stock of the situation and look very objectively at the problem in all its sad reality, before setting about the task of gently and diligently mending and healing.

Welcome to a day in Karen's brain, as it used to be…

I've woken up.
Ok, stay calm.
Hopefully it's lunchtime.
That means you have managed to get through half the day already and not eaten.
Oh my goodness! I hope when I look at that clock it says something after noon…
It's quarter to ten.
Oh no!
It's fine, let's look at it this way.
I could have woken up at 7.
So I have missed almost three more hours eating.
Ok.
But let's try and sleep again.
Sleeping means not eating.

The Argument For Changing S**t Up

Trying to sleep… brain is awake.

Why do skinny people on tv, have breakfast in bed? I wish I could have breakfast in bed.

I'd have…

STOP!

No food thoughts! Do you want to be fat and even more unattractive to others than you are already?!

Ok let's have a plan for the day.

Today I am going to do a fast, like the one I read about in a magazine article the other week.

Oh that feels better to have a plan, what a relief.

Ok am I going to eat a banana like the article suggested for dinner?

No, lets eat smooth soup for dinner because I heard some celebs have soup or baby food for dinner and it keeps their tummy flat.

Maybe some senna tablets and water retention herbal pills, just to make sure any poo or wee inside me comes out before I next weigh.

Oh god! I can feel the first pangs of hunger.

I am not going to eat because it will make me fat.

Dear Body

I am not going to eat for as long as possible so I can lose weight and look thinner.

Don't be a failure, don't eat!

When I reach the weight I want and look the way I want, then I can also start that company and write that book and go on that holiday and…

That food looks so good!

But I am not going to eat it.

…

I am so 'good' I haven't eaten all day.

I am hungry.

I want to be thin.

I am hungry.

I am scared I am going to eat.

I am scared I am going to fail at the whole 'not eating thing.'

I look horrendous, so tired.

I am definitely not going to eat.

I ate so much yesterday by accident.

I am so fat and wobbly.

The Argument For Changing S**t Up

If I don't eat for another hour, maybe then I can have half a diet bar?

If I don't eat for another three hours, then I will be a step closer to getting a 'thigh gap.'

If I eat now then I won't feel hungry.

I am hungry!

Maybe a coffee will trick my tummy into feeling full.

That black coffee has hit my very empty stomach and I don't know whether I might be sick in the next ten minutes or poo myself in the next few hours.

At least that will mean I weigh less.

…

Oh how joyful, my tummy is flat.

I am now scared to ever eat again.

I am hungry.

If I eat my tummy might bloat.

Then I will feel vile.

Then I will feel depressed.

I definitely won't eat for the rest of today.

The coffee has worn off and I wasn't sick or rushing to the loo.

Dear Body

Maybe I should have a diet coke?

I feel ill.

I feel so proud I haven't eaten now in ages.

I might not even bother with the soup or baby food, just try and go straight to sleep this evening.

I feel in control.

I am winning!

Food is not winning.

That food looks good, but I am a good person so I am not eating it.

I am hungry but I want to be worthy like other thin people.

I am winning!

…

I am eating!

Just have one bite.

I've already had three bites.

Oh f*ck.

I am hideous.

Ok, well let's just get this whole thing eaten really quickly.

The Argument For Changing S**t Up

That's it, don't taste, don't chew.
Let's get this shameful act done.
Quickly.
Okay and while we are here, may as well eat that too
because, then we can not eat for longer next time.
Good idea, let's eat that as well.
Yes, quick eat.
This is going to make me so fat.
Oh god, I am going to be so hideous.
This food is my enemy and I am cavorting with it.
Put it down.
Put your fork down.
Two more mouthfuls.

Actually four, because its a fork not a spoon so you get less per mouthful.

Ok, but stop now!
Just a last bite.
OH My GOD!!! I feel soooo full.

So full of the enemy and so full of shame and so full of failure.

I feel so full. I feel sick.

Dear Body

I look so fat and hideous.

Ooh, maybe I should be sick?

Don't be silly, people with eating disorders make themselves sick.

I don't have an eating disorder.

I have just eaten too much and that is simply because I took my eye of the prize.

So I need to get back on track.

I need to undo this hideous eating I've just done.

Being sick would sort that.

Yes and then tomorrow I won't fail again, so I won't need to be sick again, so I will just be sick today and then never again.

Ok. Oh god I wish there was a more pleasant way to get food back out of my stomach.

Why does sick have to burn?

Am I bulimic?

No.

But you have lumps of sick between your fingers and you are now retching into the loo?

The Argument For Changing S**t Up

No I am not bulimic, I don't stick a toothbrush down my throat.

Bulimic people don't make themselves sick with their fingers, do they?

Either way I am not ill, I just need to get this food out and then tomorrow I will start again and succeed.

Maybe I should order those shakes online and just live on those for a while?

Yes that's a good idea.

Oh fuck I feel exhausted and I've got a sore throat and mouth.

Don't look in the mirror as you brush your teeth.

I'm looking and I look so sad.

Have you seen how podgy your cheeks are?

Oh how do I get a chiselled jawline?

That would make me so confident and sexy.

What the hell is that on my face?

Not broken capillaries again.

I wonder if there is an easier way to be sick that doesn't involve straining until I end up with pin prick bruises all over my face?

Dear Body

Doesn't matter anyway as tomorrow will be different, I will stick to the diet.
I am so tired.
I hope I sleep at least until noon tomorrow.

***

My days varied in their extremity, but for the best part of a decade my waking thoughts were largely taken up with thinking about food or my body. Let's say I was awake for 14 hours a day, let's take four hours off each day for thinking about other things which is generous, as even whilst in conversation with others or doing other tasks I thought about how not to eat or how to change and diminish parts of my body. So that's 10 hours a day, 7 days a week, 52 weeks a year, for about ten years. That means that of my precious time on earth I have spent in excess of 36,400 hours thinking about how to starve myself and how I am not acceptable as a human being looking the way I do.

The Argument For Changing S**t Up

Strangely, when I first worked this out, the 36,400 hours didn't shock me, what did shock me was when I took those 36,400 hours and divided by 14 (waking hours) to turn them back into days again… 2,600 days. I am again crying, shaking in shock and sadness at the number of days of my life I have wasted fighting a fruitless and harmful battle with myself. I have been healthy for many years now, but still the sheer waste of my life and my time, taken up by my f**ked up relationship with myself and food, never fails to reduce me to tears and makes me so full of gratitude that that existence is no longer my life, no longer my experience.

I pray that sharing this book, opening my story to others with all its graphic and hideous detail can help others heal, even if one other person is released from the agony of hating their own body, then it will all have been worth it.

Step 3: Notice

If you can notice where you are at and take time to be aware of how you are speaking about yourself then you can change it. So, for a day just notice your thoughts, see if you can catch and be aware of your train of thought, maybe make a note of it. I try not to focus too much on this stage, simply because where you are is not where you want to be, so if you start writing your negative thoughts in a beautiful journal then they will just manifest more. Just mentally 'hear' yourself, what are your thoughts and would they be categorised as negative or loving towards your body? If you find this difficult to determine, then take the thought you have just had and mentally repeat it as if you were talking to someone you love. Does it horrify you or make you feel uncomfortable, when you think of saying that to someone else? Then the chances are it's self abuse. Noticing the chatter and thoughts that run through your head about yourself and your body, brings awareness and from awareness we can enact positive change.

Chapter Six.

Can You Really Breathe In Forever?

"The breath knows how to go deeper than the mind."
Wim Hof

I don't always sit up straight. I used to, bolt upright with my tummy tucked in, breath held, especially for photos but also just on my own, lest my gaze would meander south towards my tummy and I would see a fold or a wrinkle or anything jutting out from the vertical plane to which I forcefully tried to tense my abdomen. Now, as I sit writing this I'm slouched, which is not an advert for spinal health. But I now do this for comfort on occasion, as a measure of my progress, as a trophy of how far I've come, the gold standard of body love I have achieved. I sit with my bottom slid forward and my lower back woefully unsupported, my shoulder blades are the only point of contact with the back of the chair, I see my tummy protruding, I give it a rub like I'm making a wish. I refuse to hold my tummy in anymore. I get comfort as I write this, to prop my coffee cup on my tummy, still keeping hold of the handle, just taking the warmth from the cup. I love and accept my body to the extent now that I don't mind what shapes and angles my tummy falls into. As I look down now I think, 'you look a little bloated lower abdomen, are you ok?' Ah yes I think, I'm due on my period. 'Well you are just fine and beautiful as you are lower abdomen, thank you for housing my amazing reproductive stuff. Would you like a hot water bottle?'

This compassion, care and understanding of my body also extends to my mental health. So what is the process? I could write a whole book on the mental health aspect but I want to focus for now on the physical aspect of the process. I also don't want this to be one of those self help books that promises the moon and then you read and read but never quite feel the author says what the secret solution is, so I shall spell it out here…

The process by which to change your relationship with your body is to change the conversation you have with your body. To move from critical enemy to compassionate, understanding parent. I've given the steps to achieve this an acronym… **NNUM**

Step 4: Get NNUMing.
So what does NNUM stand for?…

1. **N**otice when you notice something.

    You will notice changes and things about your body, the reason you are reading this book is maybe that you notice too much and you spend many hours of your life 'noticing' things about your body. From now on when you notice you are noticing something about your body, say 'Ah ha! I am noticing something about my body.'

2. **N**eutralise it.

Say what you notice but without using negative language. For example, don't say 'my thighs are flabby' say 'I am noticing the top outer part of my thighs.'

3. **U**nderstanding and gratitude.

Here the trick is to change the topic of the conversation from what you previously perceived as wrong to what you are grateful for.

'Thighs, I understand that I have previously aimed much anger and disappointment at you and I am sorry, you are beautiful and wonderful' or maybe 'thighs, we walked over five miles yesterday up those hills and you are incredible, powerful driving forces for my mobility and movement, thank you.'

4. **M**ove on.

You will find that just like a bad relationship break up, crappy feelings linger, but once they are neutralised with gratitude and by using more neutral language, then you get closure from the past toxic feelings.

By taking the NNUM steps above (Notice, Neutralise, Understanding, Move on) every time we catch ourselves being negative towards our own body, we start to train ourselves out of the addiction of hating ourselves. We start to rewire our brains to love our bodies. (Google 'brain plasticity' for further info.)

Chapter Seven.

It Turns Out You Can Change The World

"Be the change you wish to see", Ghandi

Let's look at the psychology behind a destructive relationship with your body. Why do we like to watch drama? Quite simply because it excites our brain. As Russell Brand once wisely said (and I paraphrase). There aren't any computer games about providing aid, food and understanding to refugees in camps, there are however games which allow the player to play war games and shoot people.

The reason for this I believe, is not as some mid 20th Century psychological studies would have us believe, that we are innately evil as human beings. I believe instead, that we are simply addicted to drama and adrenaline. We are all so used to having our central nervous systems endlessly jangling, we have forgotten how to be at peace with ourselves. And I believe ultimately our 'default factory setting', our soul centre, is peace and that is why we crave peace but don't always live at peace with ourselves. We are addicted to the game of war with ourselves, busy shooting ourselves down and attacking our own bodies. This now is a journey to becoming more of a Mother Theresa figure in your dealings with your own body.

Stopping self hatred and self body shaming also has wider implications. On a macro level, the bigger picture, perhaps we can change social norms and language around body stereotypes, for the better?

It turns out that Heat magazine, Facebook etc (other media perpetuating self hate and body dysmorphia is available) is feeding our drama addiction brain and not our peace brain, it's driving a wedge not only between each of us as human beings, as celebrities are shamed on the glossy pages and social media sites are a hub of comparison and competition. But it is also driving a wedge between our injured, drama addicted selves and our compassionate, 'fully participating in life' selves. As I have said in the previous chapter, feeling I could only do or achieve certain things if my body looked a certain way, made me hold back, I didn't achieve or do nearly as much as I would have done, if I had always known I was good enough just as I was.

So imagine for a moment, a community or even a world, where each individual is not stifled by spending hours of their day hating themselves and believing they have to achieve a certain body image to be able to participate in life to their full potential. Imagine that tomorrow morning every living individual woke up and spent their time fully applying their energy to their families, projects, work, healing, fun and hobbies. I'm not just saying that the success of an economy is correlated with our relationships with our own bodies. I am saying the whole fabric of our society directly correlates with the relationship we have with ourselves. Our societal relations mirror the relationships we have with ourselves and our bodies.

I have realised that years ago I thought I was a compassionate, meditating, yoga going, in touch with people, type of person. The truth is I could be passive aggressive, impatient, judgmental, defensive and on occasions just plain rude. How apt that that is exactly how I treated my body, as a commodity to be perfected and used, to be abused, criticised and taken for granted. How can I expect myself to show compassion for others when I had none for myself? How can I be a fully functioning member of society, when I couldn't even look at myself without feeling hatred? I've realised if we can find compassion and a healthy, loving relationship with ourselves, we can also shine that same compassion outwards into our communities and to the wider world.

That's the macro reason to follow the NNUM steps and be your body's best friend, now for the micro reason. That is a little closer to home, in fact it resides in every cell of your body. Self love can and does change your body and in turn your health. And I feel at this point I need to flag a reminder. For those of you desperately still hoping this is a traditional diet book. It is not. The end goal is not to be thinner. There is no end goal, there is only a healthy journey. And the reason for me stating this as the logical and most desirable way forward, will hopefully be made clear by my 'horse and cart' analogy.

In this particular explanation the pink horse represents self love and self acceptance. The cart represents our 'physical and psychological self'.

Currently, most people believe and live by, the 'cart before the horse' scenario, that is, perfecting physical image is seen as a way to achieve love and acceptance of self. This prevalent belief system is evidenced in talk such as 'That's my goal weight, if I can just lose a few more pounds I'll be happy'. Changing physical image is seen as the first step, the method, the key to being able to like yourself and to be healthy.

Instead, if you put self acceptance and self love (the pink horse) first, your wellbeing (the cart) has to follow. The more love and acceptance you lead with, the more your behaviours and your physical and psychological self will head in the same direction.

Dear Body

There is plenty of evidence, (see appendix A) which can attest to the effect of thought and belief on living things, anyone who has read The Secret, followed Abraham Hicks or has any inkling of belief that 'thoughts become things', will be able to see that believing something, will achieve that very reality for you. If your mind believes something about your body, your body will respond and align itself with that belief.

Sadly, the popular response to this is 'I don't believe I am healthy and lovable and I don't love every bit of my body.' Well your body knows this and feels this, it feels your rejection, it feels your loathing. Our body in the present moment is the fruits of your thoughts from the past. You planted the seeds of thoughts and they came to fruition, some bitter, some sweet, but your mind planted them, even if they were originally comments by someone else, which you started believing too. Your belief system, however you acquired it, is the lens through which you experience your reality.

So how do we break this cycle of believing our current manifestation and replanting the same seeds? Well, we can't do the same thing and expect a different outcome. We need to lovingly plant different seeds, we need to stop drawing on our current reality as we perceive it. We need to imagine, we need to believe….We need to fake it.

Asking you to 'fake' loving your body, may not sound particularly groundbreaking, but it is in fact a powerful tool to start to experience the feeling of loving your physical body. We need to plant different thought seeds in order to produce different results from those which we currently have. We need to play with the law of quantum physics that like attracts like, we need to harness the power of our minds, which are basically energy waves (as is everything in the entire universe) and get to grips with the fact that if we are thinking a certain way about our body, then the law of quantum physics dictates that the cells of our body (also made up of energy waves) will be created in the way you believe yourself to be.

The quantum level view of our mind, body connection shows the futility of putting the cart before the pink horse, it's like saying 'when I am thinner/musclier/lighter/etc then I will love myself' and the law of attraction will deliver exactly that, an experience of not loving yourself and constantly being on a journey of waiting to look a certain way so you feel you can love yourself.

Faking some self love, is a leg up, a change of direction and mentality. After a while faking it, you start to find a glimmer of belief that you look healthy, strong, thriving, beautiful, glamorous, funky, unique or just very much owning your own fabulousness. Then the law of attraction mirrors those new beliefs right back at you. The energy waves of your new 'self love' neural pathways will resonate within every cell in your body. The positive cycle will start to spin a little quicker and more easily, as you start to automatically view yourself as lovable, attractive, worthy etc. And importantly, your psyche starts to learn that the body you inhabit is a safe and kind place to live.

(To get more in depth understanding of the law of attraction see some of the resources listed in appendix A)

Step 5: Believe the change you wish to see!

So far we have,

Step 1, written a love letter to our body.

Step 2, got in touch, literally, with parts of our body.

Step 3, noticed and started to become aware of how we are talking to ourselves.

Step 4, moved the noticing into the full process of NNUM.

And now **step 5**…

This is basically a souped up version of step 2.

Hug yourself or hold a part of your body and say these or similar affirmations

'my goodness I am healthy'

'my body assimilates what it needs from my food and ejects anything else'

'my body is in sync with the huge amount of love I have for it'

'everyday I feel safe and secure and all is well'

Fake it until you make it. These affirmations I've introduced here might feel like you don't quite resonate with them yet but don't worry, it is important to remember that for some months I had to become an actor, I had to imagine I was playing the role of a person who loved my body. That way, initially I was faking it, but then suddenly and I can't remember the exact point, I realised I was believing what I was saying.

Chapter Eight.

Treat Others How You Wish To Be Treated.

"A single act of kindness throws out roots in all directions, and the roots spring up and make new trees."
Amelia Earhart

This chapter tackles the sad but very real social phenomenon of trash talking others and perpetuating negative language around food and bodies. The simple solution would be for the whole world to stop doing it, but its not that straight forward. I became aware of increasing negative talk around bodies and food, both in the media and in everyday talk, I realised it was fuelling my issues and undermining my progress, especially in the 'fake it 'til you make it' stage. I also realised that as much as I was a victim of negative talk, I was also guilty of it.

What I found interesting when I started on my journey of noticing (step 3) is that body shaming and self shaming has become so ingrained in our everyday speech, that we have stopped seeing it as strange or wrong, our ears no longer hear the damage until its too late. And it isn't just about ourselves, its about others too. I have become a Jedi Master at spotting negative talk in a social setting, I can even sense it coming now, just based on someones body language. Early in my recovery I could feel the trash talk brewing in myself as colleagues poured over a magazine which states that we should decide which celebrity has the better thigh gap or the most cellulite. Now however, I simply *notice* and then walk away, remove myself from the situation, like a recovering alcoholic who finds themselves in their local pub eyeing up the rows of spirits, walk away, seek help. Help for me, if a therapy session wasn't immediately available, came in the form of my affirmation cards, a useful tool especially in the vulnerable recovery stages. I wasn't part of a support group, so apart from therapy sessions my go to solution when I felt challenged was to find a quiet place, to sit, close my eyes and repeat my affirmations over and over like a fervent prayer.

My job as cabin crew for an airline, meant that not only was I in a role which judged and praised certain appearances and gender normative stereotypes. But also put your body through sleep deprivation, jet-lag symptoms, exposure to radiation, lack of oxygen, close proximity within a confined space to pollutants, viruses, bacteria, strangers and colleagues, many of whom I had not met before each flight. Oh and the farting of said strangers. Enjoy your next flight!

Dear Body

Exhaustion and jet lag is the perfect bedfellow for cravings, especially sugar, caffeine and alcohol. What do you do after work, when you have been verbally abused by complete strangers for 12 hours because their inflight movies weren't working? It's time for wine. And when it's 4am and you have to be alert in flight to medical situations, aircraft security, fire precautions and provide service with a smile, all whilst having had 40 minutes sleep sat bolt upright freezing cold on a crew seat? Time to eat your body weight in chocolate and wash it down with a few strong coffees.

I paint the worst picture here, but it is still a very real aspect of the context in which I was trying to get well. Faced with the above lifestyle, most crew I knew were either 'trying to loose weight' or 'obsessive about health/exercise.' The result is that a vast majority of chat between crew was about someones diet which was, 'really working for them,' or whether they should be 'naughty' and have another one of the 25 chocolate desserts left over in business class. So very regularly in flight, I would retreat to the toilet and lock the door, not to make myself sick any more, but to take some deep breaths (if the deposits of the previous visitor to the toilet, didn't prohibit nasal breathing!) and read my affirmation cards. I changed them as I felt the need to, but my first one said

"I am worthy, I am loved,
you, dear body, are perfect just as you are."

I would patrol the cabin with trays of juice cups, walking the aisles much more than required, just to remove myself from toxic conversations amongst crew, about bodies and food. And the result, was that I started to emotionally detox, my mind started to feel clearer. I had begun to not allow the poisonous thoughts in, so the symptoms of poisoning in my mind and body started to ease. Prior to this, if I had heard chatter about the latest diet or about how someone had lost weight, I would forget everything and be totally immersed in ferociously trying to find out every detail so I could know the 'solution' which had worked for someone. I was an addict. I am an addict. My drugs of choice? Self shame, image competition and food control.

I am well into recovery. The time for you to feel that you can 'walk into a pub and stay sober' might be different to me, we are all different. I still occasionally have to carefully monitor my mind's thoughts, keeping an eye out for a negative and harmful thought, but I can now stay around the chat. I don't partake or participate, I just smile, letting the words sail past me. And interestingly, the chatter has subsided, I now have different conversations. In line with the law of attraction, it seems I am now attracting more beneficial, interesting and funny topics of conversation.

Step 6: Create affirmation cards

Write out the affirmations from Step 5 use colourful card and pens or just write them on a piece of scrap paper or screenshot them and save them as your phone screensaver. Either way, make them part of your daily life. When the need arrises take a minute and read them, use them as your anchor point to a feeling of self compassion.

I couldn't write a chapter about how we talk to each other without including the topic of Social Media. Just as how we talk to ourselves has influence, how we are influenced by the words and actions of others, presents itself so strongly in our online lives. Part of the journey towards loving your body and healing the world around you must include how you relate to online content, particularly social media. It's time to move from comparison to compassion, and from competition to cooperation. Social media is awash with anxious and fearful energy, pitching individuals into a toxic game of competing to be heard and comparing everything from cars to physiques.

Social media isn't all bad, it can be a fabulous and powerful tool, however it can get hijacked by beings in such an egoic dark energy that its magic abilities get forgotten. Part of my recovery was to close all my social media accounts and delete them permanently. For many of you this will seem very drastic, however I would argue that a holiday away from social media is one of the most cathartic and empowering things we can do in our modern world.

Just as I have explained about negative or abusive thoughts influencing our physical and emotional health when they are inside our own heads, allowing toxic language and opinions into our personal spaces and sanctuaries, via our smart phones, works in a very similar way. Before the internet and social media, we could leave people's comments and judgements where they belonged, outside of our homes. Now the opinions of others can infiltrate your emotional wellbeing as soon as you unlock your iPhone. Historically, I had such an anxiety reaction to Facebook that even seeing the blue colour of the Facebook branding and the f symbol, made me sweat and my heart rate increase.

Treat Others How You Wish To Be Treated

The best way to ensure that your online 'socialising' isn't damaging your wellbeing, is to make sure you are compassionately parenting yourself. Maybe start by reducing your time on social media, set a timer limiting your browsing to 15 minutes a day. Another way to critique and reassess the way social media is influencing your self worth and self love is to ask yourself, is my social media content representative of wider society and the wider world? The answer is probably no, because social media is steeped in privilege and assumed norms, furthermore the algorithms will only show you more content and opinion which is aligned to your previous interests and preferences. Initially we could think this is handy, we get information familiar and interesting to us, belt fed straight to our senses. However, the problem with this is, if our interests aren't serving us, or aren't for our highest good, we get more of what isn't good for us, delivered to the palm of our hands. And our brains perceive it as true reality.

Dear Body

If you once followed someone on social media who liked to present themselves airbrushed and conforming to certain ideals which aren't necessarily possible or desirable, then the site or app will show you more and more of this type of content, before long your brain will be even more convinced that everyone on the planet, apart from you, has managed to drive a Bentley convertible, drink cocktails in Dubai and get their entire body to be an even tanned, unblemished complexion.

I think most of you can imagine the type of content I am referring to. I do not say this with judgment of any beings, I say it because I have found that materialistic, body idealistic content, to be the most damaging to my psychological health. It is so powerful that even now when I use social media I have to self parent the content very carefully. The TikTok speech claiming to be 'self help' and a few seconds in is describing what you 'should' be eating or not eating. If I find myself watching something like this I go straight to search something totally unrelated such as horses or kittens. Or I close the app and walk away from my phone. Either way, you will feel in your gut when content isn't right or doesn't resonate with your new found self love and acceptance, and you can take action to remove it from your personal space.

A holiday away from social media, is ideal if you know on some level that using social platforms triggers more anxiety than it solves. A good idea is to delete the apps from your phone and then after a designated amount of time, maybe a few weeks or months, choose one platform and carefully curate who you now want to follow. Some fabulous people have inspired me with their content and no nonsense approach and made me feel it is safe to follow them, as I allowed social media back into my life.

I've listed some of them here.

@meganjaynecrabbe

@thecompletioncoach

@lucymountain

@megan_rose_lane

Dear Body

@i_weigh
@jess_megan_
@michellelelman
@thebirdspapaya
@aliciamccarvell

And the fabulous human who designed the cover of this book @stephaniechinnart

Chapter Nine.

Pray, Love... Eat. The Importance Of Attaching Love And Positivity To The Food We Eat.

A wonderful elderly Indian lady I knew, prayed while she cooked, it's commonly done in certain cultures, religions and spiritual practices. And oh my goodness her food tasted divine, pardon the pun! When I remember to, I waft my hands over my meal or drink and imagine it being infused with love and good energy. I'm sure many of you will instantly see that this is a sensible and intelligent idea, to think of our meals as sacred, to energetically imbibe our food with positive energy. However, some of you gorgeous souls will either think I'm wasting my time or that prayer and positive affirmation around what we consume is absolute nonsense. So for those of you who need evidence as to the veracity of a claim, I will endeavour to include it here.

Attaching love, not guilt, to food is absolutely pivotal to recovery. My brain transcript (chapter 4), revealed that, in the past when I did eat, there was so much guilt and shame going on around the act of eating. This not only was an unhappy and unhealthy way to eat, but I have since learnt it changes the chemistry of the food. We have explored how negative self talk and thoughts affect our biology, but our thoughts also affect our food.

If possible, take some time now to look at the videos in the following YouTube links. These are examples of experiments showing the impact of how we talk to plants and food.

'Bully A Plant: Say No To Bullying'.
https://youtu.be/Yx6UgfQreYY
'The Impossible Rice experiment'
https://youtu.be/zvShgttIq7I
'The Power Of Words' Jovanka Ciares
https://youtu.be/6GpH3dbSMok

Dr Masaru Emoto, carried out many experiments with water, some of which can also be viewed on YouTube and indeed there is plenty of information about his work on the internet and in the books he wrote. His findings show the profound effect of human consciousness on water, thought patterns and sound waves are seen to change the shape of frozen water.

Therefore, just as with the ice crystals in Dr Emoto's experiments, how we think about and talk about our food, creates a response in our food and our body on a cellular level and so is pivotal to our wellbeing. And here's where it gets really interesting, if how we talk to and think about our food has such a profound effect on it, then negative talk is basically helping us deteriorate, it's making us sick. Attaching guilt and shame to food is negatively deteriorating the food we eat which, in turn fails to nourish or benefit our body.

My wonderful yoga teacher and mentor, Claire Missingham wisely states, 'While Cooking, blending, serving or creating food in any way. Chant Mantras. Send love to yourself and anyone sharing your food. The Sadhana Kitchen is a yogic and preventative approach to living and eating mindfully, from a place of deep love and appreciation for exactly where you are right now.' (Sadhana means mindful and dedicated practice.) So it's not just how we talk to ourself which is important, it's the emotions and thoughts we attach to our food which also affects our wellbeing and our ability to thrive.

Step 7: Get friendly with your food
Next time you make a cup of tea or cook a meal or even eat a meal someone else has cooked, take a moment to have a little chat with what you are about to

eat or drink. Feel gratitude, feel positive thoughts and see the food as divine and a gift for your body. Say an affirmation such as, "I am so grateful for this food which nourishes my body." This is very similar to step 2, but instead of smiling at and touching a part of your body, you are thinking loving and grateful thoughts towards your food.

Still need further proof of the power of your words and thoughts? Create your own experiment like the ones on YouTube, maybe with a plant or an apple, get creative and see for yourself the power of your words, thoughts and intentions on everything around you and possibly everyone close to you too.

Chapter Ten.

"UgUg" We Are More Cave-Person Than We Realise.

I haven't forgotten I left you in suspense about 'Zen Tummy', way back in chapter 1. I think the best way to describe zen tummy and what it is, is to explain how to get it yourself. Once you feel it, you'll understand it and it will be easier to live more and more with zen tummy.

I'll start at the very beginning. Many thousands of years ago, during the era of the first primitive humans living here on earth, they didn't have 'diet' foods or meal replacement shakes. They didn't have diets of any kind, they wouldn't have understood the concept of a diet to lose weight. What they did have, were times of starvation or lack of food and they did have times when there was ample food; a good hunting trip, clement weather which helped plants and berries to grow. Many thousands of years later, a meal replacement shake and the concept of a diet, is widely recognised. To many a diet is the next new thing that is going to rescue us and save us from a life of feeling shame. We forage and hunt through social media, magazine articles, tv adverts and friend's chatter, in search of the diet which is going to work. However, diets don't work and here's why.

Picture the scene. It's a Friday, you've come home tired and have eaten half a packet of chocolate biscuits, devoured a tub of ice cream and made a good start on a bottle of Sauvignon Blanc. Due to societal norms these things are labelled 'bad' and so the self shame and hatred is cooking up nicely. You search for a solution, let's make a plan to undo the self harm through food, let's go on a diet! 'Right! On Monday I am going on a diet where I will restrict what I eat, and then I will be thin and then I will be beautiful and then I will be loved… but that is for Monday, until then, pour me another glass and break out the Doritos!'

Your conscious modern brain is happy with that supposed solution and your evening continues. However your primitive brain, the inner chimp who doesn't understand diets, just hears a communication that in a few days there will be a lack of food. Thousands of years ago, survival depended on being able to look at the weather and the surrounding environment and predict the availability of food and where to find it. Survival depended on being able to predict, prepare for and adjust biologically, should there be a lack of food. So upon hearing there will be a lack of food on Monday, the primitive brain doesn't think, 'it's ok, there is food available, its just we are going on a diet, we are choosing to reduce our food intake,' it doesn't understand diets remember. So what the primitive brain thinks is, 'we have detected a lack of food resources in the near future, we will take steps to protect our survival.' The steps your primitive survival brain then takes are automatic, biological and cognitive. It realises that due to a future lack of food, it needs you to eat more now, whilst there is food available, so 1) it ups your hunger. 2) It makes you think only about food, and 3) it stores in your body as much fat as it can from what you eat.

Therefore, even thinking about starting a diet will make you more hungry, make you obsessed with thinking about food and will make your bodies fat stores nice and full, ready for that starvation period you have told your primitive brain, is looming in a few days time. This is the very reason why when you are fixated on dieting and loosing weight, you will constantly think about food and eating. Your primitive brain which has for thousands of years ensured your survival, is being tricked into thinking it needs to save you from starvation, and all because it doesn't understand diets. It can't comprehend that you would willingly starve yourself even if there is food available.

The solution, is to work with your primitive survival brain, by telling it there is plenty of food available. The first step is to put aside the idea of dieting and instead give yourself permission to eat whatever you want, whatever your body needs and continue to do this, one day at a time, for the rest of your life.

I know, those of you who have lived with food control and restriction as part of your daily life are quite possibly freaking out at what I've suggested. That freak out is exactly what I had to overcome as I sat in the therapists room and then ventured to M&S food to buy and eat anything and everything I wanted. And don't forget that I had no idea it would work, I hadn't even dreamed a glimmer of the primitive brain theory. I just had to trust. And most importantly, I just had to remember that I didn't want to live the rest of my life at war with food and at war with my own body. It took me many months of having to remind myself, again affirmations were invaluable. I would look at a menu or open the fridge or step into a supermarket and I would have to stop the old thought patterns in their tracks and sometimes even say an affirmation out loud.

'you can eat anything you want.'

'There is an abundance of food available and you can eat whatever you want.'

'Your body takes only the nutrients it needs from the food and ejects the rest.'

'I am in harmony with my miraculous body and I lovingly nourish it with food.'

When I have described this theory to people, a common reaction is 'my goodness, if I gave myself permission to eat what I wanted, I just wouldn't stop eating until I burst'. My answer to that is, that is only true when your primitive starvation brain is in control. When you are desperately trying not to eat the biscuits, you end up eating ALL the biscuits, because the restriction you have placed on eating the biscuits, has triggered your primitive brain into thinking there is a lack of food imminent. Remember it doesn't know that there are thousands of biscuits available to you, it only hears that there is a restriction, a lack of food, in this case biscuits. So if you give yourself permission to eat whatever you want, your primitive starvation brain will get back in its box and when that happens the three primitive starvation reactions are reversed.

1) It settles your hunger.
2) It stops filling your brain with obsessive thoughts about food and gives you back your head space to consider other things, like say, writing a book!
3) It stops storing fat from what you eat, instead your digestive system assimilates only the nutrients it needs to maintain your bodies functions.

"UgUg" We Are More Cave-Person Than We Realise

So, as I stepped into M&S food that day and gave myself permission to eat anything I wanted, what I had done, without knowing it at the time, is put my primitive starvation brain back in its box. I had told my primitive brain, for the first time since I was a child *'there is so much food here and there always will be'* and my primitive brain's predictable response was, *'If there is so much food then you don't need to feast, especially as there will be lots of food available in the future too, so we'll just have a bit of this and that, then you get on with your day, don't worry about food'.*

When your primitive starvation brain is back in its box, your tummy will suddenly feel satisfied, you reach a place of equilibrium and it is such a peaceful place to be. And that is why, as I stood there in M&S food, the hum of the fridges, the chatter of people and the beep beep of the tills, I suddenly felt very calm, very zen. For the first time in as long as I could remember my 'self criticising shame brain' and my 'primitive starvation chimp brain' had stopped their full volume, constant argument. They had laid down their weapons, stopped their war of words in my head and gone for a snooze, I had found peace. I had made my peace with food. And this is Zen Tummy.

Living with Zen Tummy, takes breaking the habit of saying 'no' to yourself, it also takes a leap of faith that your primitive brain will back off and go to sleep. But please, take that leap, you will find that your hunger and body shape finds it natural equilibrium, its optimal place. After discovering zen tummy, my body shape changed quite dramatically, as anything stored under the misapprehension of impeding starvation, dropped away. I found I was looking more like myself, I found my body was fiercely intelligent at knowing what I needed and when. Some days I craved water, tea and apples and my food intake was low, other days I would wake up hungry and have six meals in one day. I no longer labelled foods as 'good' or 'bad', I just simply noticed what I fancied to eat and then I ate it, sometimes this was chips and beans with sweets and crisps, sometimes this was fish and steamed veg.

"UgUg" We Are More Cave-Person Than We Realise

This continues to the present day, my hunger ebbs and flows with the physical and hormonal demands of my body each day, and I have learnt to listen and to trust. If I am eating a chocolate dessert at work and someone says 'my goodness where do you put all that food you eat?' I just smile and take their email so I can send them this book when it's published. If I haven't felt hungry and am still pottering around, and others are eating, they sometimes say to me 'you're good, you have barely eaten all flight.' Again I just smile and offer to send them this book when it's published. The one thing I don't do is take on board their comments, there is no 'good' or 'bad', only an abusive or compassionate relationship with food and with yourself. It isn't the food which is unhealthy, it's your beliefs about the food.

I use NNUM to stay mindful and present with my zen tummy and to not awaken the primitive starvation brain.

Here's how NUMM works with food and hunger.

Notice: My body is telling me I'm hungry, don't judge that sensation, just breathe and notice.

Name and Neutralise: 'Ok body, you need nourishment, what do you fancy to eat? You can have whatever you want'

Understand: Food is what sustains my body, any hunger is a reaction to internal or external environments. By this I mean, maybe internally you are due on your period or externally you have been rushing around a lot, or maybe you just weren't hungry yesterday. Either way your body is asking for food and that is fine.

Move on: eat mindfully and with gratitude, joy and love for the food and your body, then carry on with your day.

Step 8: Go food shopping and give yourself permission, or if the food is already in the house, give yourself permission to eat it, as much or as little as you want. The whole time keep in mind that this is not a binge, you have to tell your primitive chimp brain that ample food will be available to you for the rest of your life. You must love and send positive thoughts to your food and savour and enjoy it. Listen to your tummy, stop if you want to stop eating, start again if you want to start. Trust your body to know, without its chimp brain interference, what is right for you, what your body needs.

Chapter Eleven.

Addicted To ~~Food/Fear/Shame~~/love

"Shame corrodes the very part of us that believes we are capable of change"   *Brené Brown*

In time it is possible to move towards self love. But I have realised that my ongoing recovery from being addicted to self hate and to self harm using food control, has required that I understand the nature of the addiction cycle, why and how it self sustains and how to isolate it at the root.

Addicted To ~~Food/Fear/Shame~~/Love

I see the addiction cycle as operating like this…

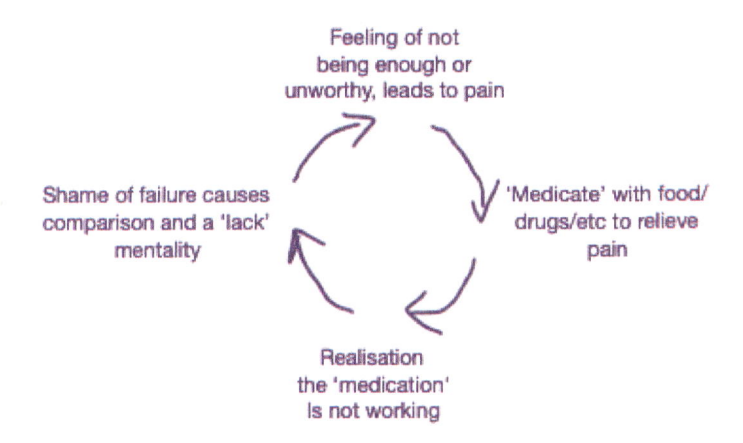

```
        Feeling of not
        being enough or
        unworthy, leads to pain

Shame of failure causes                 'Medicate' with food/
comparison and a 'lack'                 drugs/etc to relieve
      mentality                                 pain

            Realisation
          the 'medication'
           Is not working
```

There is a form of pain from the feeling of not being good enough. In order to get relief from this pain we medicate, however the medication itself does not serve us, it comes in the form of excess or self harm, be it cake or crack, or anything we are using to get temporary relief from the feeling that we are not enough as we are. This temporary seduction, the lie we continually believe, that the cake or the drug is our cure, soon shows its ugly side as we realise we have been tricked again, we have taken the 'medicine' and still ended up in the same place we started, or ended up feeling worse. We feel failure for not 'solving' our pain, we feel we have not achieved, not arrived at where our life should be, so we feel shame at this failure, at still being in a place of not being who we feel we should be, at not feeling we are enough. This shame and pain, leaves us desperate for a 'cure', desperate to feel something other than pain, and by the time we look around again for some relief, or for the answer, what we are addicted to has again donned its mask of illusion, it is again conning us into thinking that it holds the answer. And so the cycle repeats.

And this is why the diet industry, and the 'weight loss' industry and even the concept of dieting itself, is so lucrative and has been for so long, it is also why it doesn't work. Because it is, knowingly or not, based on the addiction-shame cycle, it is offering us the cure, it is suggesting that it has the answer to not feeling good enough, of coming up short when compared to others. But what it doesn't tell you is that the feeling of not being

Addicted To ~~Food/Fear/Shame~~/Love

good enough, the idea that comparison is healthy and constructive, is peddled by the commercialisation of gossip, body hating and shaming of others.

Many diet companies actually use comparison as an advertising tool, *'look at this person when she wasn't worthy and hated herself. We cured that and now look how happy she is'*. It is pure and utter nonsense and it ruins lives. You can weigh, count and measure and you may acquire what would look to be societal weight loss 'success'. But have you addressed the root cause of your pain? If you feel you have, then I send you love, I congratulate you in finding peace and contentment and I wish you well. But I would argue that losing weight does not unlock anyone from a life of dieting. And a belief system that equates self worth and love for ones own body, with a certain physical appearance, is not sustainable or desirable. Ask yourself this question, have you ever been totally happy with your body? If the answer is yes, then ask yourself. When you were totally happy with your body, did you live in fear of it changing?

Dear Body

This is the problem with dieting, is that any perceived success is merely a house built on sand, one day the tide will come in and the foundations will shift. Stronger foundations are required in order to live in peace and loving harmony with your body, proud and grateful for your body. It cannot be based on appearance, it has to be based on a psychological and emotional belief that you are worthy just as you are.

Addiction feeds itself, it is self sustaining, however crucially it requires all elements of the cycle to be present. I am reminded of early school lessons on the triangle of fire; ignition source, fuel and oxygen are all required for fire, take one element away and there is no fire. I believe the same is true of the cycle of addiction, by removing an element of the addiction cycle, the pattern can be broken. The element I tackled was 'shame', through therapy I made a decision that whatever pain I felt in my life, however my body looked and however others behaved towards me, I was not going to be ashamed of who I was or how I looked. Brené Brown does ground breaking work in this field and I highly recommend her books.

I have realised that the reason I had such a toxic relationship with my own physical body and with food, was because I was so afraid of feeling shame. So addressing this fear and knowing that by tackling shame head on, I had already won the battle. I had chosen to be the nurturing protective parent to myself rather than the shaming abusive parent. I had chosen to say, 'body you can look exactly how you look, I love you just as you are' and 'I am going to continue to look after you unconditionally, to nourish you lovingly with food, to care for you in the way I know you deserve.' Just as a loving parent would protect their child from harm, abuse, judgement and shame. I had decided to do the same for myself. With the shame removed, there was no fuel for me to self harm or medicate with food, no drive to starve or feast or vomit. I would feel emotional pain and know I needed to address something, change something or just give myself some time, stay in my pyjamas, chat to a

Dear Body

friend, practice some self care and self compassion and know that, as with everything… this too shall pass.

Chapter Twelve.

I Hear Ya' Tummy!

My constant fear of getting or being 'fat', meant I had constantly lived in fear of the natural evolutions of my body. I would poke, prod, judge and hate every bit of myself which didn't measure up to some unobtainable 'media' ideal of the human female form. I was at war with my body, instead of listening to and working with my body to find a harmonious existence. Once I had started to (via fake it before you make it) talk lovingly to myself and to my food, I realised I had also started to listen more. As my self parenting with compassion really started to take root, my self talk evolved even more and I realised that my body was desperately trying to talk back, desperately trying to provide me with information, so I could make even better self-parenting decisions.

Previously, I had cut out foods and restricted myself with the pure goal of weight loss and social acceptance. Now with a total free run of food shops and restaurants I began to see how my body and my thoughts were affected by what I ate. I was confused at first because I was eating mindfully and with love and I felt better than I had my entire adult life. But my energy was still low and I suffered horrendous bouts of bloating and IBS. Early in my recovery I noticed my swollen, bloated tummy one day and just as the negative thought was forming in my mind I grasped it, kicked out the horrid self talk and quickly dug around in my mind for a loving thing to say to my tummy. "Tummy," I said, placing a hand on my distended abdomen, "you know I love you unconditionally, you seem in pain, is there anything I can do for you?" My stomach gurgled loudly, I doubled up in pain. Previously, I would have been in a flail about my

I Hear Ya' Tummy

non-flat stomach, swearing food was never going to pass my lips again, but now I was resolved to find the answer to my stomach's woes, like a parent seeking treatment for their poorly child.

Warm water and stem ginger, kept coming into my mind, bizarre as I had never eaten stem ginger before, but I bought some. I sat sipping warm water, nibbling stem ginger and hugging a hot water bottle to my tummy. The pain eased, I could feel the spasms in my tummy easing. I had helped my poor tummy regain equilibrium, but I wanted to know what had caused such pain and discomfort in the first place. I sat quietly, and asked the universe/angels/god/anyone, for help and to show me the answer.

The next day at a therapy session, recounting my bout of depression and tummy issues, my therapist asked if I had ever had testing for gluten intolerance or coeliac disease. I hadn't, and I was nervous of 'cutting out' a food incase it triggered my needing to control, diet or manage in any way what I was eating. Even writing down what I had eaten for breakfast at that time, could trigger endless food diaries, starvation bouts or adopting another fad diet.

So with trepidation I went to the doctor for a coeliac blood test. It came back inconclusive, but whilst waiting for the results I had decided to remove gluten-containing-foods from my diet, I still ate bread, cakes, pasta, I hadn't stopped allowing myself anything, I had just decided to use, gluten-free versions of these foods. There are no words to explain the life changing impact this had and continues to have on me even almost ten years later. I suddenly, within a week of removing gluten, had so much energy, my depression had all but disappeared, my skin was clear, my leg cramps stopped. I realised I had been feeding my body something that didn't resonate with it, something it didn't like. From then on I decided to listen to my body, to be aware of changes in my physical and psychological wellbeing and just notice, just **NNUM**, when a food hasn't resonated with me or when my body is telling me something.

Notice: Tummy looks bloated or feels unwell.
Name/neutralise: 'Beautiful tummy, I love
   you, how can I help you feel well?'
Understand: Listen to your 'gut instinct' (it's
   called that for a reason) what does your
   tummy need or what food does it not
   resonate with? Seek professional advice if
   need be. (See appendix C for resources.)
Move on: Compassionately do what your body needs and then get on with your day.

It is a fact that certain foods unique to you, can be out of resonance with your energy. I use my instinct, trial and error and energy testing (more about energy testing in the next chapter) to guide my compassionate decision making around foods that will help and heal me. I have found that if I don't listen to my body and what resonates with it then my emotional wellbeing suffers too. And this is where the old habits can be tackled from both angles, now your body and food is treated with love and respect and a desire to understand, then the three of you (mind, body and food) can work in harmony. Your psychological wellbeing will benefit too, not only from a physical equilibrium, but from an understanding that you are safe and nurtured and any emotions which arise will be lovingly addressed and if necessary resolved, rather than disregarded and attacked with an arsenal of self harm and body-hating shame.

Being a loving, non-judgemental parent to yourself, means viewing the ever evolving body you inhabit as a beautiful miracle, something to be amazed and impressed by. Just as I mentioned that I sometimes sit slumped and rub my tummy, fluctuations and changes in your body are temporary states, it is not a battle to be taken on. We cannot and should not be at war with the miracle of being alive, the miracle of ageing and the miracle of being conscious experiencing souls in the wonderful and diverse bodies we all inhabit. Periods, hormonal fluctuations, biological and psychological reactions to food, air travel, anxiety, food intolerances, allergies, illness, in all these situations our body needs a compassionate response, in order for us to thrive and live in harmony with ourselves.

If we live with a dread and a rejection of our body and all its day to day changes and cycles, then we will feel trapped in our clothes and fearful in our bodies. The truth is, without our paranoid thinking, our bodies would be in perfect balance no matter what shape we are. It's our relationship with our bodies changing state that can set us off kilter. The fear of rejection because we are seeing ourselves on the precipice of 'failure', of not being fashionable, of not fitting in, which causes us pain. We are all different shapes, we are all beautiful. Living in that love and understanding for our own bodies, will bring our health and wellbeing into a place of harmony. And will ensure our bodies, hearts and minds can experience love and life to the fullest.

Chapter Thirteen.

Good Vibrations. How To Test Your Resonance With Food.

The aim of this chapter is to take our relationship with food back to a more basic and functional foundation. To strip back some of the emotions around food and eating that don't serve your greater good and to instead see food, eating and digestion for what it is, a very clever series of chemical reactions.

One day at a time, I have a healthy relationship with food. It is however a constant skill to hone, not one that takes up my every waking thought any more, but occasionally I take a moment to be aware and to reflect on what I could improve on to enhance my wellbeing. Something that comes up for me is that I still don't chew my food enough. I haven't yet addressed it, it's like an act of subconscious rebellion, the last vestiges of me not wanting to command or restrict my behaviour around food. During my horrendous years battling myself and food, I spent a while doing the 'chew food X number of times before you swallow it' diet. So I think now I'm cautious to change or count or adjust my natural eating habits. And let's just say I eat as if I've been given a trough or a nosebag! Not the whole meal, I love putting my cutlery down and having a breather, but when I am eating, it's fairly speedy.

I reflect that there may be some dregs of shame in the process of eating still, or maybe being cabin crew for so many years, I learned to eat quickly before someone interrupted me asking for a gin and tonic, or asking where the toilet is, or when we are going to land. But whatever the cause, I feel my eating will slow down in time.

However, taking our time when eating, is important. Firstly, shovelling food down doesn't give us time to chew and chewing is the start of the digestive process, important enzymes in the saliva start the digestive process even before you swallow, so if that step in digestion is skipped then we are missing out on important chemical reactions which our body needs to complete. Secondly, it shows that there may be guilt or shame attached to the process of eating.

When a certain food starts its journey through your digestive system, the amount of nutrients you end up getting from the food is going to depend on three key points. The nutrients in the food before it enters your body. The health of your gut and therefore its ability to absorb nutrients from the food. And whether or not you resonate with the food.

Good Vibrations

The first two points are worthy of whole shelves of books and medical journals in themselves, so I shall leave those topics to those much more informed than me (suggestions of titles for further reading are provided in appendix C). The third point, whether or not you resonate with the food, might sound strange, but as mentioned earlier our thought vibration effects food and our body. This is because everything in the entire universe is made of energy, the chair you are sat on, the skeleton and muscles keeping you sat on that chair, the neural pathways thinking about being sat on the chair, all at their smallest components, are waves of energy. We see some of this energy manifest with our eyes through reflection of different light energy waves, we hear sound waves of energy, that plane over head, a favourite song on the radio. Some energy is less visible, your wifi silently and without you being able to see it, travels from your router to your laptop or smart phone. All energy is working around us and within us, even if it isn't always visible to us.

Our food is also made up of energy waves and it's this fundamental scientific premise that I have learnt to combine with the age old idea of our gut instinct. No coincidence that it's called our 'gut instinct' as it is the energetic heart of our unconscious wisdom. We can start to use our gut instinct to determine if our body needs or likes a particular food. We can start to sense the energy of a food and ask our gut if it resonates with it.

This is a deeply intuitive process and we are all capable of it. It has been selected for as humans have evolved over thousands of years, our ancestors had community elders and spiritual gurus who sensed the way forward for a group or guided decision making. In a similar way those who foraged and prepared food for groups learnt to avoid certain foods, they used feedback from the body, from objectively looking at what the food did for them. But most importantly they cooked from the heart, they intuitively chose what they used to fuel themselves and their community. As we have seen earlier, cooking from the heart imparts a wonderful energy into the food which makes the food more beneficial to the body, as does eating without shame or guilt attached to the food. Choosing your food via intuition, instead of via predetermined social rules or the goal of loosing weight, helps you see what will bring your body into equilibrium. What will resonate with you and nourish you.

A good example of this is my experience of cranberries and chips. Using the often peddled paradigm of 'good' and 'bad' food, I think we can all identify which food would traditionally fall into which category. However, my body doesn't resonate with cranberries, they give me a tummy ache. That doesn't mean they aren't a nutrient rich food source, many people will resonate with cranberries and they will get key nutrients from them. I am intellectually aware that I can't live just on chips, however potato resonates with my body really well. I can eat chips and I feel fit as a fiddle, no adverse effects. So the key, here is to change how you choose your food. Yes, you are aiming to fuel and nourish your body, but you are aiming to do that via an inbuilt energy detection system you innately possess, not via commercially determined ideas of what are 'good' and 'bad' foods.

I'm going to share the exact mechanism by which you can check if a food resonates with you and your unique digestive system. I have in the past had a full food intolerance blood test, I found it very useful, because it gave me a window of clarity to start to sense more closely and intuitively how each food effects me, and to what extent it resonates with me. Instead of choosing certain foods so I lose weight, I choose foods that resonate. This not only means food is more enjoyable and is providing precious nutrients to my body, it also provides another way to heal my relationship with food. It provides an alternative and constructive way to choose what I eat. The more you choose foods which resonate with you, the clearer your ability to intuit what suits your body or what your body needs, will be honed.

So how do we do this, firstly through the process of NNUMing, by noticing fluctuations and changes in our body with compassion and non-judgement we can learn what causes dis-ease in our body, we can notice when we eat something and it doesn't sit right. Secondly, and most importantly, you can feel the vibration of your food as a way to help you ask your body whether it resonates with you. Just like you try on a pair of trainers before you buy them and go running. You can ask your body if the particular food feels comfortable for it.

Step 9:
How to check if a food resonates with you.
Sit comfortably, if you like, follow a short guided meditation to get in the zone. Or just focus on feeling stillness in your body, take three deep breaths with your eyes closed, then bring your palms together at the centre of your chest, push the palms together and lift your elbows so your forearms are parallel to the floor. Now rub your hands together, keep rubbing, be vigorous, you will feel the heat building. After about 30 seconds, stop

rubbing, still the hands together at the heart centre, take a deep breath and move your hands very slowly apart, until there is a slight gap between your hands. Focus on the space between your hands, you may feel heat or tingling, you may see brightness around your hands. Now take a food, it can be anything, maybe be a piece of raw ginger or a crumpet or a tomato or a cashew nut. Place the food item in the palm of one hand and hover the other hand about two centimetres above the food. Say out loud *'does this food resonate with me?'* Whichever answer comes into your head is the correct answer.

You can cross-reference your findings with eating the food and seeing how your tummy reacts. What you will discover is that your body, your intuition, will say *'no'* to the same foods that seem to cause upset in your body. The step outlined in this chapter might feel very natural to many of you, especially if some form of mindfulness, meditation or energy work, is already part of your life. If you feel this is a little too 'woowoo', then I get how you would feel that, but play around with it, have fun with it. Let the proof be in the pudding. This journey is about learning how to play with the concept of food and how we choose it, rather than letting food rule you.

Chapter Fourteen.

Craving Freedom From Cravings.

Having read the previous chapter, you may be thinking that body intuition will say no to raw kale and yes to chocolate and it might, in fact my body does prefer chocolate. My digestive system resonates best with kale when its juiced or cooked, instead of raw which can make me a little gassy, oh who am I kidding, it makes me inflate and then deflate like a balloon, with full trumpet and percussion sound effects! But I think what you may be worried about is that instead of hearing your intuition, you will be hearing your cravings, or you will be hearing your inner 'food police' voice.

Let's tackle these potential doubts now. The inner 'food police' voice, the judgements of whether food is 'good' or 'bad' should be dissipating as you continue to use the previous steps and in fact, it's a case of being a 'good cop' to your previously negative and harmful 'bad cop' thoughts. Cravings are a different thing, firstly they tend to be triggered by; emotional attachment, social conditioning, habit or nutritional deficiency in the body. So let's look at each cause of cravings in turn and I'll explain how the steps outlined in this book will help you work with, rather than against your cravings, to understand them and to eliminate those that do not serve you.

The emotional and social link to food and eating habits is looked at a little later on, however it is so important that I am covering it briefly here too, specifically in relation to cravings. Beautiful soul, as you entered this lifetime you came with a DNA blueprint, you came with a soul purpose, a Dharma, a Kismet. However, from your first day on this planet your whole physical existence revolved on a human level, around survival. As helpless infants we have evolved to ensure our survival by gaining attention from caregivers, so that they respond to our requirements when we are too young to be able to resolve our needs ourself. It is no coincidence that a baby learns to smile so early in their development, it's in order to bond with and give positive feedback to their parents, as soon as possible. Such attachment cues become intertwined with our emotional relationship with food.

Our upbringing and the layers of habits we added as soon as we were allowed to walk down to the sweet shop on our own, elicited food choices which either stuck and became habits or faded away into the past. The ones which became habits and we are talking from a practical level here, are serving us on some level. They are ensuring that we find some calm and some head space by using familiarity . The universe and everything in it is constantly changing and renewing. We as humans however, like to think we have created a form of settled familiarity which is ours to control and maintain, a protection from the unknown, the unknowable and the unpredictable.

Habit stifles the unknown, it serves to avoid venturing into territory for which the knowledge to deal is not necessarily readily available, especially pre internet. The problem is that habits around food especially, don't always serve us. Being not only samey and limited in their variety but also detrimental in how they control us. Habits become cravings when they become a reflex which our brain has come to expect.

Let me illustrate with the following exercise, complete the following sentences with whatever comes to mind.

Tea and…
A nice glass of….
…and cream
…. for breakfast.

I would bet that the majority of us got similar answers for each sentence.

Our food habits are steeped in social conditioning and habit.

This is why many of us feel comforted by large corporate food and drink chains, it's familiar, it's perceived by your brain as predictable and therefore, it is considered by your brain to be something you can crave. Because if you have had a certain burger before, your body can ask for one again. Rinse and repeat, your brain loves to find familiarity and Mr McDonald and other similar food corporations, know this all too well. We all have habits and we all have triggers which we associate with certain foods and this is centred around our brain loving the familiar, it feels safe with things which are known.

These habits also mean that our nutritional uptake stays very much the same, even if you eat a very balanced diet, I can guarantee that your nutrient levels are not all as they should be. Because as much as we would like to think our nutrition can be stabilised and then forgotten about, our bodies need a constant adjustment of nutritional uptake. Our body on the whole does this itself, but only if the nutrients is available in the first place. If a particular nutrient isn't available to our body and it is required, then in the first instance our brain and tummy will put in a request, in the form of a craving. You might think it's strange that you suddenly start craving something quite particular, like lemon for example. If you ignore such cravings your body will continue nagging you with cravings a few more times. Then if you catch a cold due to a lack of vitamin C, for which your body had asked for lemon, you take medication for the symptoms, but leave the underlying vitamin C deficiency unaddressed. After a few months and your body has recovered from the cold, you notice that you are craving orange, you reach for the orange squash (orange flavour, not the real thing, but it's what you've always bought) and you go about your business, your skin is feeling a bit rough and sullen, you keep picking up sniffles and you feel lethargic all the time. And through all of this you are ignoring cravings thinking they are always a bad thing, when in fact your body is requesting what it needs.

Trying to ignore cravings without understanding the root causes can leave you missing vital information your body is trying to communicate to you. We can discover if a craving is habit and old conditioning or it is a useful piece of information from your body by looking at the context of the craving your body has come up with, which helps decipher whether the craving is our chimp brain squawking or our intuitive brain. We can then pair that with other information your body is giving you outside of the craving. I guide you through this process in step 10, on the next page.

Understanding cravings from a nutritional deficit point of view will depend on your understanding of foods and their nutritional value. This is why I got help to start with and its why I educated myself on food and nutrition. It's something I continue to learn about and I find it has without a doubt changed my quality of life. I realised in my recovery that time spent staring at social media, wondering how many people are loving my posts, could be better invested understanding how on a biological and nutritional level, food works with my body. Eating is something we all have to do, and so many of us don't even understand the reason why we are eating what we are eating. Whether we are eating out of habit, or because we have made an informed, joyful choice to respond to the needs of our body.

I whole heartedly suggest you seek professional advice for any symptoms or illness you have, alongside this there are some fabulous nutrition professionals out there. Become a detective and see food as a wonderful fuel which can be studied and understood below a surface level. I do also believe in supplementation and intolerance testing, see appendix C for further info. Addressing any longstanding nutritional deficiencies with a professional will help give you such a firm foundation from which to NUMM cravings, this process will help steer you towards freedom from fearing your cravings, to a place where you can harness the power of them.

Step 10: NNUM your cravings.

Notice: Just notice the craving, stop, take a deep breath and have that awareness that you are engaging your human and not your chimp brain.

Name/neutralise: State the craving "I am craving peanuts." Try not to say negative phrases like "I would kill for" or "I'm gagging for".

Understand: This step is often more than just a statement as it might have been before. It's the step where you get your compassionate parent hat on, but you also become a bit of a detective. The aim is to be as objective as you would deciphering someone else's cravings for them. The previous steps should have helped you to get into the flow of objectively gathering feedback from your body and mind. Using the example of peanuts, when I last craved peanuts my response was, 'my skin seems dry, I haven't had much protein today and I enjoy the taste of peanut butter'. I could objectively see the possible reasons why I had craved peanuts and I could see its nutritional value. Also peanuts are a food which resonate with me.

Move on: I ate a gluten free crumpet with peanut butter on top, I moved on, no guilt, no judgement and with plenty of self loving thoughts towards the food and my body.

Chapter Fifteen.

The Emotional Link To Food. "Be A Good Girl, Have One More Mouthful!"

Eating everything on your plate, only getting dessert if you have been 'good', *treating* yourself to something yummy because you deserve it, are all very usual childhood habits thrust on us by our parents, which unfortunately have produced an emotional link to food and craving. Such early parenting techniques and social learning comes sometimes from historical necessity. During World War II, waste was not an option, it was a case of eating everything on your plate so that nothing

The Emotional Link To Food

went to waste, so that no one starved. I really dislike waste, I believe in a zero food waste policy, for both financial and environmental reasons. It takes resources to produce something, it takes your earned money to buy it, so no one wants to see it go to waste. That said, we are not human shaped bins or compost heaps. We do not have to squeeze and cram everything that is on our plate into our mouth.

The echos of 'one more mouthful' and 'eat your greens' should now be laid to rest, you are now a grown up who can eat *anything* you want, whenever you want, however you want, you do not need to rebel against or comply with childhood acquired eating habits.

There are many alternatives to dealing with leftovers on your plate, when your newly acquired 'zen tummy' informs you that you do not want to eat any more of your meal. My favourite option is to just put my plate on the side in the kitchen with a cover on and then see if I want it later. I find that when I am having very zen tummy days I eat two small dinners, one dinner feels like too much in one go, but I get hungry an hour later and go for the second half. Another option is breakfast; yesterday as I sat typing the previous chapter in this book, I took the cottage pie remnants from the night before and ate it for breakfast.

As a child I would share with my sibling, or be told 'you won't manage a whole one', so the largest ice cream was rarely available to me, and that's understandable, I would have wasted it. But my childhood brain continued to crave this idea of buying the 'biggest' or the 'most' of something. So fast forward to adulthood and I would walk into a coffee shop and buy the largest coffee possible, with skinny milk and sugar free syrup, but always the biggest. You see society i.e. most of the food and drinks industry has played a very clever trick on us, they have triggered our inner childhood brain and told it, *'you are now allowed the biggest portion on the menu, with all the syrups, sprinkles and toppings'*, whilst simultaneously saying to our adult, restricting, dieting selves, *'we can make something for you that is the biggest but also has the word skinny/diet/slim in it'*. Many marketing strategies sell this supposed solution to a conundrum which does not need to exist in the first place.

Our child self wants to be treated, wants to know that we have been 'good' and so we replicate the ice cream our parents would treat us to, our inner child wants food as an indicator of love, as reinforcement that we are worthy and loved. Our brains have been hardwired to crave a treat, because that's what we were given when we were 'good' as a child. Translated this means, we have been taught that food equals love and acceptance.

We grow up and this childhood learning is then overlapped with a new societal learning, that love and acceptance from others is acquired by having a certain appearance, by our body being a particular shape, with sticking out bits only in some places and tucked in bits in specific other places. We are also told that to acquire this particular body shape and therefore the love and acceptance of others, we need to not eat, or to only eat particular things. This illustrates that two contrasting templates of acceptance become welded on top of each other in our brains. We learnt a pavlovian reaction to certain food as reward for being 'good' and then get told a few decades later that if we want acceptance as an adult in this world, then we better live on thin air and spinach juice. The two ideas go to battle in our minds and yoyo dieting is born, or in my case, the binge and vomit cycle is born.

The perfect illustration of our emotional link to food, comes from my coffee shop experience before I was in recovery. Picture the scene, I'm a young adult and I'm in "Moonbucks" getting a drink which tells the child in me I've been a good girl; it has all sorts of toppings and it also tastes hideously sweet. But I've asked for it to be made with skimmed milk and sugar free syrup, so it also makes my people pleasing, adult brain feel like I'm conforming to the idea of trying to be slim enough to feel socially acceptable. The drink makes me feel sick, but I also like the taste. At first I feel relaxed and then I start to feel guilty, as the milk gurgles around my tummy, I realise I am now convincing myself that I should have had a green tea because that would have been 'better'. I sit digesting the drink as best my body can, I feel shame, I feel guilt, but I know tomorrow I will be back for another and of course I will always ask for the biggest size, and I will make sure I drink every sip. Simply because no one is going to tell me I'm not allowed the biggest size and because once I've bought it, I won't want to waste it, I'll finish it all, I'm a 'good' girl. My chimp brain would start to run riot as I wonder if I can be sick to make myself feel better.

So there it is, an illustration using the largest coffee chain in the world to show what happens when childhood learning, mixes with social conditioning from the diet and fashion industry and manipulation by certain aspects of the food industry and their marketing strategies, which in turn collides with an eating disorder.

Dear Body

Looking back now I can see its a perfect sh*t storm, into which someone has introduced a fan on max speed!

At the time I just felt pulled in different directions, I felt that the answer was out there, that the answer would be provided by the industries and professionals who know about these things, surely a major supplier of diet products would be trying to help me? Surely global governments, advertisers and pharmaceutical companies have my health and wellbeing in mind? And even when I became cynical that they did, I instead attached my 'pleasing everyone' good girl status to slightly more out there diet ideas. I ran (a lot) everyday. I ignored the extra nutrients my body would need because of all the running and I tried to fast, I lived on herbal tea or soup.

But still, I never quite got to the stage where I felt society was giving me the pat on the back I required to stem the feeling of lack, the feeling of not being good enough. What society did provide me with was pictures of supposedly 'happy', smiling women, who were radiating an image that said, *'look at me, I'm just so happy in my own body, because I have a flat stomach and slim arms and toned legs and because I am wearing a tiny bikini on the cover of this magazine. I have that ultimate feeling that I am successful and happy and… do you want to know how I got here?'* The model would silently whisper to me from the cover of the glossy magazine. I would be beyond myself to know the secret to their happy, glowing appearance, desperate to know their 'secret formula'. I hadn't found the solution in other diets, but I always believed that this new diet plan or idea would be the answer, would be the ultimate solution which made me feel good enough and made me feel successful that I had made my body perfect.

How wrong I was. I can still plug into that feeling, I can try the feeling on again, like an actor returning to a character they used to play, pulling on the outfit they wore in a famous scene and feeling how the character felt. Feeling the desperation, the constant searching for an answer, the constant waiting. I remember endlessly waiting for the day I felt whole, waiting to feel that others couldn't hurt me, waiting to not feel afraid, hoping I could look at my body and feel proud. I remember feeling so trapped, so tired of waiting for the day I felt acceptable. And each morning when I realised my battle to change my body to a socially acceptable norm was still ongoing, still my present, still my existence, that realisation each morning, brought a feeling of sadness so strong, that it echoed and ached through my body and soul.

This cycle of wasting our life, waiting to be told we are good enough is so futile, for two reasons. Firstly, no one ever truly feels they have got there, all those celebrities/actors/musicians/etc shown clutching an award or living in that vast house, I can guarantee achievement will not quash any feeling of unhappiness or any feeling of not being good enough. Secondly, once you do decide you are worthy, without needing your external appearance to necessarily conform to anyone else's rules, then you discover a deep compassion, an ability to care for yourself and others which is so powerful, so pure, so humble, so humane and so beautifully human.

Step 11:

The next step is to educate yourself about where your food comes from, how to cook your favourite dishes, how to cook dishes you have never cooked before, eat more, eat less, play around with your zen tummy. Try and step away from eating in ways that your childhood or society have prescribed. Put your cutlery down mid meal and pick them up again. Let your zen tummy guide you as to whether you are even hungry. Play, without fear, feel freedom in your relationship with food, have fun.

For example, as a child I always had breakfast before school, now I've realised that even though I really enjoy traditional breakfast foods, I am rarely hungry before 11am. Even if I awake early, it takes 4-5 hours for my tummy to wake up and ask for food. At which point I might have gluten-free toast or a full fry up breakfast or some leftover cottage pie.

Dear Body

Follow your instinct, from the perspective that there is no lack or limit to what you can eat, or when you can eat, you can have everything and anything. Focus on this mentality to make sure that you are eating to fuel your body and not because your chimp brain has panicked and initiated starvation mode or because your inner child has remembered childhood programming or because your vulnerable 'wanting to be accepted' social self has decided that a certain combination of food or way of eating will make you look the way society has decided you should look. Also, and most importantly, as you play around with different foods and ways of cooking, get rid of anything with the word 'diet' or 'skinny' on it which is in your house. Whether its a yogurt or a cookbook, evict it from you life (unless you prefer the taste).

Set yourself free with food, have faith in your ability to compassionately choose for yourself and nourish your body and love your body. So that your miraculous body starts to reflect that love it is being shown, starts to show the health of the loving energy that is being directed at it and to it. Remember those plant and rice experiments. Make sure you are talking and thinking about yourself and your food in a way which will make both resonate with vibrant life force. Feel the love!

Chapter Sixteen.

Forest Gump Didn't Run To Lose Weight.

"I just… felt like running" Forest Gump

Do you ever think about how you move your body? Do you ever move your body in a way that would be seen as sports/fitness/a gym activity etc? Do you ever move your body to lose weight? Do you ever move your body to change its shape? Do you ever move your body to feel like you fit in? Do you ever move your body to compete against others? Do you ever move your body to feel better? Do you ever move your body, just so other people think you are 'good' for working out?

I would guess that most people can answer yes to some or all of those questions, but what about this question. Do you ever move your body just for the pure joy of it? Like when a cat or dog has a 'mad five minutes' dashing around for what seems like the pure fun of it.

I would always find it interesting, when I signed up to the latest gym that I thought was going to be *the* gym that succeeded in making me finally happy with my body, none of the tick boxes under the title *'reason for joining the gym'* gave the option *'for fun'*. Looking back, all the gym memberships I ever acquired just made me feel like obtaining my 'skinny happy' life was like being on one of those treadmills, a never ending task. Hard work, sweaty, boring, repetitive, ego based and always focused on an end goal. Do this to get that. Eat this to be that. None of the weight loss focused exercise I ever did could be described as joyful. Occasionally I enjoyed a bike ride, or

I felt smug when I had worked out, or I liked the endorphin buzz after a HITT class, but it was never joyful. And the reason it wasn't joyful was because just like a diet or eating plan, an exercise regime or fitness craze is selling you something. It's selling you hope. It's selling you the hope that you can be happy, it's selling you the idea that you will have a body that you can be proud of, a body that will make people unable to ever reject you ever again. It is selling you a new beginning and my goodness us yoyo dieters, us body haters, we love a new beginning and a fresh start! We are addicted to the idea that next week or even tomorrow will be the first day of our transformation, and our transformation will end with an applause of love, acceptance and attention from others.

I applaud anyone who wholeheartedly wants to enhance their life by finding wellbeing, even looking for wellbeing is a brave and wonderful step. But wellbeing is not endless amounts of time staring at a view that doesn't change as the treadmill belt trudges around beneath our feet, wellbeing is not '*I should*' or '*I must,*' wellbeing is not shrinking our body to a silhouette which 'fashion' deems acceptable.

Wellbeing is movement without that constant inner chatter of critique, wellbeing is movement where you find yourself in the flow, wellbeing is movement for the pure unadulterated joy of it. At some point we forget this, we knew as children that movement for the pure joy of moving was fun and blissful. But now, we attach so much to movement. It's time to strip away the end goals, the PB's, they can be added again later in recovery if absolutely necessary, and importantly if they add to the joy of the experience. I still don't measure my movement. I also don't schedule, create routine or planning around moving my body. My obsessive running timetables are a thing of the past. I sometimes go for a run with my partner and his iWatch measures how far we've run, but it doesn't matter to me how far or how fast or what pace I've run. There is no end goal, no strategy, because I am not moving my body for any reason other than the present moment joy of being in my body as it moves. Movement is a gift for which I am forever in gratitude, feeling glad, feeling amazement at the miraculous movement of my body. Movement is a privilege.

Finding a contentment in the present moment with the movement of our body, nurtures our inner child and it also creates a new found sense of freedom, we do not have to move our body to pre-determined routines, plans and goals. We can just move for movements sake.

The first time I danced sober as an adult, was at my first retreat, I was still battling with my body and with food and the retreat leader led a session where we closed our eyes and as a group just danced, we couldn't see each other, because our eyes were closed, but still it took me a while to warm up and not feel self conscious. We were encouraged to just let ourselves be nimble and fluid and instinctive, just move in any which way that felt good. I started to get the hang of it and after a while I was flinging myself around with abandon, giddy with the freedom.

At the end of the dance session, we had a sharing circle, each of us confiding something we had learnt that day. I shared the fact that I couldn't remember the last time I had danced without being under the influence of alcohol. In fact I don't think I had danced sober since ballet class, which I gave up at about 7 years old. Since then as a child, I had just sat nervously if there was dancing at a party, or not gone to the party at all. Then as a teenager, I had found alcohol and that had been my solution, my brave juice, which 'allowed' and supposedly 'enabled' me to dance.

I am still not a very dancey person, I'm not one of those people who seeks out dance scenarios of any genre or guise. But I still felt it was such a loss that from a small child dressed in her ballet outfit, to an adult of 28, I hadn't felt the joy of dance, without being inebriated. And so now, in celebration of my new found freedom, I move my body with joy and abandon and I don't care who's watching.

Step 12: Move. Close your curtains and find privacy if you need to, turn the music up and fling your body around with pure abandon. No previous dance experience required.

Whether this is something which you learn to enjoy or whether, like me, you only ever appreciate the novelty and the feeling of movement and know it will never be classed as 'dance' by the outside world, it doesn't really matter. What matters is that you feel fluidity and movement in your body without any rules, without any prescribed reason. This also addresses any addiction to perfectionism which might be stifling creativity and it is a brilliant way to reconnect the 'me' inside with our physical body. It reconnects you to freedom to express, freedom to be without boundaries, freedom to allow and freedom to be in joy, freedom to not need a plan or specific outcome.

Forest Gump Didn't Run To Lose Weight

Now we are all limbered up, feeling a little more free and adventurous in our physical body, never again to be that person just gently nodding a head or tapping a toe along to the music, start to feel movement in your body in a direction you have never thought about before, wiggle like a worm, move like a robot, watch as your limbs get moving and shaking. Smile! Welcome to the joy of moving your body with freedom.

Chapter Seventeen.

The Gift Of Another Day.

"It is through gratitude for the present moment that the spiritual dimension of life opens up."
Eckhart Tolle

As I began to realise that I didn't have to spend my life endlessly waiting to feel good enough or to look a certain way to participate fully in life, each day started to take on a new feel. Instead of being tired and exhausted at the prospect of another day to be dealt with, I became excited at how I could shape and explore my day and therefore my life. I started to see my time and my life as more and more precious.

Is there an activity or sport you have always wanted to try? For me it was Brazilian Jujitsu, in the end I didn't enjoy it enough to continue, but I tried it and I enjoyed stepping out of my comfort zone, I found it fascinating to relate to my body through a contact sport. It made me realise that contact from another person to my body is either medical, emotional or sexual. Utilising my body in such a physical contact way was so different to any other sports I had done before, it showed me yet another aspect to my relationship with my own body which I had either been oblivious to or had been ignoring.

I often try new things and dance like nobody is watching as part of my recovery and my new found gratitude for life. Part of the reason for this is because repeating the same activities, eating the same foods, constantly moving my body in the same way day after day, all in the majority of cases, because of the desire to lose weight, was a double sadness. Not only are we spending hours, days, maybe years of our precious life trying to minimise and shrink our miraculous bodies, we are also limiting our experience to known and repeated activities and sports. We are missing out on new adventures, the excitement and thrill of pushing our boundaries, we are also spending our life doing stuff that we potentially don't want to do.

Instead, let's move our bodies in a way that makes us happy, let's explore uncharted territory, let's stop repeating the same thing over and over. The only people who want you to be stuck in repetition and paying for it are gyms and diet companies. Let's stop the rinse and repeat, and start experiencing our bodies through the joy of novel movement, with the sole focus of being in a place of wellbeing by moving with joy and compassion. Time to stop the grind and the gritted teeth, time to take away that finish line which even when crossed we place further away, or which we never allow ourselves to cross, so we never take time to celebrate what we have achieved. We need to stop making our poor body a victim of our fitness regime. We need to stop the *'I will be happy when I can or when I have'* and start just enjoying the movement, for the sake of the movement. Start to revel in feeling our limbs move, feel the bliss of stretching our backs, feel the thrill of gliding through water, feel the connectedness of team sports, the community and the fun and the joy that can be found. Life is not a competition, its an opportunity to experience, an opportunity to hone our abilities as a compassionate, sentient, mindful soul.

Finding joy and gratitude is a practice which can spread beyond feeling and moving our body. For example, I practice mindful gratitude when I'm loading the dishwasher. *'Thank you for the abundance that enabled me to afford this machine, thank you for the clean safe water which is pumped straight into my home for me to use, thank you for all these utensils which enable me to prepare and eat anything I want. Taking this time to clean and organise my home in any way is an act of self compassion and I revel in providing myself with this sanctuary in which to live.'* No longer just the task of loading the dishwasher, but an act of gratitude, a chance to stay present, humble, and never taking a single day for granted.

Step 13:

Today, set reminders if you need to, as you go about your day, start to think about what you are grateful for and do at least one thing you have never done before. Never done a cartwheel? Give it a go. Never done a team sport? Sign up. Never been to your local park? Give it a go, enjoy, be in joy, be in gratitude, being alive is a miracle. And most importantly, each day start the habit of looking in the mirror and saying to yourself,

*'I am grateful for you,
I love you.'*

Chapter Eighteen.

Knowing Me, Knowing You. How Our Relationship With Our Own Body And Self Is Pivotal To All Our Other Relationships.

"Your task is not to seek love, but merely to seek and find all the barriers within yourself that you have built against it." Rumi

I consider myself a recovering perfectionist. I used to place such pressure on myself to conform, to be accepted and to be 'good'. I had a wonderful upbringing and very loving parents. They did exactly what they needed to do, to help ensure my survival, they taught me how to be 'good' and conform, they taught me how to fit into society as they know it. They also taught me how to have fun and be a bit adventurous, so luckily there was a balance there. But by nature I am a people pleaser, my default state is, 'how can I serve you, so that you think I'm a good person.' As part of my recovery I have had to totally remove this statement from my brain and then reinstall 'how can I serve others?' However being of service to others is different to being in servitude. My service to others is now underpinned by a brain document called 'Self worth and self care.' This is because I have realised that if we grow up to be people who hang our very existence on the praise and acceptance of others, then we are f**ked until we have a serious rethink of our worth and our priorities.

Imagine you are a boat in a stormy sea without an engine or a sail, tossed around, occasionally crashing onto rocks, never understanding why you can't seem to sail in the direction you want to go and never seeming to find respite in a harbour. Occasionally, you pair up with another boat and they might have an engine or a sail. They throw you a rope so you grab hold of it and they pull you along, you are so grateful that you start to fear the other boat letting go of their end of the rope.

And then sometimes another boat comes along, you tether your boat to theirs, but after a while, you realise that the boat who has offered to save you, doesn't have an engine or a sail either. You are both adrift, ending up bashing into each other with each wave, dragging each other in no particular direction.

By tethering ourselves to any passing boat, we start to see the sea as more dangerous than it might otherwise be. We remember the time we were tethered to another boat and it dragged us against rocks seemingly out of control, we become fearful that we need to be rescued, that we need other people in order to survive. By not seeing ourselves as worthy of a sail or an engine we forfeit our ability to steer our own boat.

You are worthy of your own sail, your own engine, or both if you so choose. No one else can fix your boat, no one else should tell you your boat needs fixing. It's your choice whether you have a sail or an engine and you should never let anyone steal your sail or engine. For anyone who hasn't guessed, this metaphor is about your self, your body and the wider world around you. It's about your self worth and how you relate to others.

This rather long boat metaphor serves to illustrate how dangerous, pointless and hurtful it can be to allow yourself to be adrift, to allow yourself to be waiting for outside confirmation from others that your body is acceptable, that you are worthy. The important thing here is not how your boat looks, its not how big, small, old or new it is. It's that you allow yourself to steer your boat based on your own means of propulsion, you sail your boat through life taking responsibility for the path you charter and for the decisions you make. No one can tow you forever and you shouldn't have to tow someone else forever.

To get our engine going and our sail up we need to look after and nurture our boat. It's important that your boat is sea worthy, that you give it the care and attention it so dearly deserves. Paint it and adorn it, present it however you want to, it's your boat, the important thing is to make sure you take time to lovingly keep up its care and maintenance. There are many reasons to do this.

Firstly, if you are a parent or you become a parent, then your children will watch how you take time for self care, whether its a hot bath, a pedicure, a no holds barred dance around the kitchen to your favourite music, or whether you take time to make and enjoy a particular meal. Let them see you taking at least some time each day, being present, being mindful, being aware of the fact that it is important to look after your body, to be nurturing and caring towards your wonderful miraculous body. From a very young age, babies mirror their caregivers, whether it's a smile, a fearful reaction or knowing how to unlock an iPhone! They imitate. They will imitate the self care and the self worth practices they witness too. They will imitate if you rub your tummy and say *'I love my wonderful tummy,'* they will also copy you if you grab at a part of your body and say *'I hate my…'* or *'I am so fat'* or *'I wish I had…'*

Self worth, self love, practiced through self care, nourishing and nurturing your health and body, is so unbelievably important because the habits and beliefs you have for your body, will be passed on to the next generation. If your children watch you on a diet rollercoaster (and don't think for a second you can hide it from them), then they will believe that that is how an adult should treat their body, how they should relate to their body. It also becomes the way they judge others, it becomes, they assume, how others view them. I had been holding hands with a boyfriend, when I was about 19 and I remember thinking, *'goodness I hope he doesn't think my hand is fat!'* Instead of connecting with and being present with that person, I was consumed with a narrative about what that person might think of my body. Have they noticed I'm slimmer today because I've starved myself for two days? I can't sit there and chat because he'll see that my tummy doesn't stay vertical and rock hard when I sit down. This negative self talk in relation to others, perpetuates a feeling of not being good enough, of not being worthy of being with another person.

As I recounted from a therapy session at the beginning of this book, I started to believe that when I felt rejection it was because the other person hated my physical appearance as much as I did. I didn't see that maybe the relationship was meant to end anyway, that maybe rejection is a healthy part of the ebb and flow of human interaction. I also didn't see that maybe I was being rejected because they weren't ever really with the real authentic me, they were with a preoccupied, self hating, version of me. How could I have been good company or even a good listener, a good lover, a good friend to anyone, when my prime concern was how awful I thought my body was and what people thought of my body. Self-rejection, made me an inauthentic and selfish person to be around and to be with. I had little time to really listen and so I never heard what people where trying to say. I never saw past my muffin top over my jeans or the spot on my cheek, so I never saw the beauty of the world around me.

I didn't accept myself as loveable so I tried to fixate on someone I thought was lovable. This is, for many people, one of the unconscious reasons why they are with a partner, because they make them feel more socially acceptable, more worthy. For many people it isn't even the person, it's the relationship status itself. *'In a relationship,' 'married,'* these labels seem to carry a social kudos, which a lack of self worth deems will be the perfect balm, the ultimate solution. The trouble is, these labels are not a cure. Our feeling of not good enough or our disgust at our own beautiful bodies returns just as the confetti is swept up, or as we eat our first cake having starved and dieted for months to fit into a wedding dress that didn't ever need to be so small. We have hung our hat of self worth on someone else's existence, we have tethered our boat with no engine or sail to someone else's. For many people in a relationship, they unconsciously want something out of it, be that security, social acceptance or self worth. If both parties are equally gaining and are happy with that, then your boats tethered together might work. But a relationship doesn't have to be based on that.

During your initial recovery through the steps outlined in the chapters, if you are in a relationship, ask your partner to bare with you, healing our relationship with our body is the only way to a more peaceful life experience, but changing old habits and ways of living or relating to ourself, can cause others to initially wonder what is going on. However, after a while, you will suddenly realise that you have more capacity for other things in your life. Remember all those days and hours I calculated that I had spent thinking about food and self hate and changing my body? Through this process we are taking back that time and that emotional capacity. And the beauty of that is that we can share this time. We can be more present when a partner is talking, we can really hear others instead of just thinking about how to respond, we can encourage and support our loved ones without fear that we need to guard against them becoming more attractive to others, we can be wrong and be ok with that. Because if we have our own boat with a sail or an engine and someone sails off without us, because they reject us for some reason, then we can enjoy the sailing trip on our own for a while.

If we give ourselves permission to be wrong or to make mistakes then that is a significant step in recovering from perfectionism. If we learn that we do not need to be perfect to be loved and accepted by others, then the beautiful thing is, we allow others to be imperfect too. We understand how difficult it can be, to be in this human existence and we acknowledge that everyone is doing their best. We learn to trust, because our very existence does not depend on being tethered to someone else's boat. We learn to nurture others, from a place of pure love, because we have insisted on adequate nurture for ourself. We can love unconditionally, because we feel worthy of it being reciprocated.

Step 14:

Remember how we learnt to look at or touch a part of our body and just notice something, to start feeling gratitude for how that part of our body is so miraculous and clever. For this step pick a person in your life, it could be a parent, it could be a partner, a sibling, or a friend. Focus on them in your mind and pick something about them, it might be their hair, their humour, something they have done. Start to feel the compassion and love for that particular aspect, feel gratitude. Your brain might interrupt you at this point, especially if this is a totally alien practice for you, that's ok, notice what the brain interrupts with. Whatever the criticism you are levelling at others just realise that that is also the critique you are holding against yourself too. For example, if your brain interrupts with the thought that they never listen, I would suggest that your mind is so busy thinking that they don't listen, that you probably aren't taking the time to hear them. So if your mind wonders to a criticism return to a positive aspect to smile at and be grateful for. Sit with that feeling of gratitude for a few minutes each day. My partner and I call it a *'gratitude shower,'* we think of one droplet of gratitude and as the feeling and things we are grateful for perpetuates in our mind we realise its like feeling gratitude and high frequency vibration raining down on us.

Say *'thank you'* and *'I love you'* to your loved ones every day. You are extending to others something which you are learning to give yourself, unconditional love.

Safety note: Abuse lingers and hides within some relationships, self harm and harm of others tends to hide in the shadows of privacy and intimacy. When you are treating yourself and your body in a 'loving parent' nurturing and compassionate way, others should of course behave in the same way towards you. Unfortunately, some of the people we have allowed to be near and dear to us, were chosen or allowed in, at a time when we lacked self care, self compassion or self worth. Many people and partners will be supportive of new found self worth and many will flourish in the unconditional love and compassion shown to them. However, some will not be able to get past their fear, some will have deliberately chosen you because they subconsciously or otherwise saw that you maybe didn't have a sail or an engine when you met, and they knew they could tether a rope to your boat and drag you in their direction, at their speed and through their storms.

They may not adjust too well to you having your own sail or engine. This is not a judgement, I send them love, for they are being shown their lack of self worth in the most difficult way, against their will. They are being told by you healing and having self worth, *'look how you and I have decided that our self worth revolves around both of us being tethered together crashing around in a storm of self hate and rejection.'*

That partner who becomes fearful of your self compassion, didn't pick up this book, they didn't ask for the status quo to change, so they may become very scared of changes they see in you. In order to keep you from acquiring your sail or engine, they may use manipulative and abusive behaviour. I cannot tell you what to do in this situation, other than to say, bring to mind the loving nurturing parent behaviour, which I mentioned before, imagine a small vulnerable child and the compassion and respect they deserve and ensure that you are treating yourself in that way and by making those compassionate parent changes for yourself, you will make the right decision to step away from those who are too scared of you having self worth and self compassion. (Further help can be found using the resources in Appendix D.)

Chapter Nineteen.

Fight, Flight, Feast Or Famine.

Often when we are suffering from anxiety or panic, it is because we have subconsciously told our nervous system that there is a problem. A theory I have developed during my recovery, is the idea that our physical body spends a lot of time scared. And strange as it might seem, I believe in many cases our physical body is scared of our psychological mind. We are literally threatening ourselves, we are often the ones peaking our own adrenaline and self protection mechanisms.

To illustrate, I'll repeat a phrase I heard a dear colleague use about herself.

"I'm a fat cow"

Now imagine you are walking down the street and a complete stranger walks up to you and aggressively spits in your face the words *"You fat cow."* I'm sure you would feel upset, angry, concerned, confused. But how would you feel physically? Shaky, sweaty, stressed, maybe your heart would race, your confusion and anger would make your jaw clench. Maybe you would recoil, step back, try and run away. This is our fight or flight response. Even reading that scenario may have triggered a physical, emotional, chemical and energetic response from your incredible body. It is so powerful, it is what has saved us humans from death for thousands of years. Our brain perceives threat, in this scenario it's another person being verbally aggressive, and our brain and body immediately unravel a series of plans for how to deal with the threat. Adrenaline ups our heart rate and puts our body on high alert to run, to take flight away from the threat. It also stimulates our aggression and fear so we take on feelings and strength in order to fight. It's a heady cocktail, it's powerful, life saving stuff.

But what if the threat never goes away, because the threat, the aggressive, hurtful, attacking voice, is coming from inside our own head. When we speak hurtfully or negatively of or to ourselves, when we have lack of compassion for ourselves or even lack of acceptance of any part of ourselves, we are basically throwing our primeval selves, in a cage with a snarling life threatening lion. And because our self attacking thoughts and our flight or fight response are both coming from our brain, we are locked in with the threat. The perceived threat to our lives is internal, we are living with it, day in day out, this is not only exhausting as we are constantly on high alert, it also becomes detrimental to our health on a longer term basis.

There is much research now into how modern life is peaking our stress levels, so we are stuck in a fight or flight response and in turn maxing out our cortisol levels.

Dear Body

Cortisol is your body's main stress hormone, if your body is on high alert, cortisol acts to shut down other bodily functions such as digestion, immune and reproductive systems. Conditions including adrenal fatigue, autoimmune response diseases and chronic exhaustion may follow from the body living in a state of adrenaline stress over an extended period of time. Many of us are living in a constant fight or flight scenario. We are not creating environments and lifestyles which allow us enough time to feel safe, to allow our adrenaline to level out and our bodies to feel at peace. Gratitude, self love and acceptance counteracts our bodies stress reaction, allows us to practice peace in our own mind and body.

Living ever ready to run or fight, takes a lot of energy, in order to account for this we have evolved a clever little system to deliver the energy required whilst in fight or flight response. We crave sugar and fat, we switch from peacetime zen tummy to a full on war footing and this carries with it a variety of immediate responses, all of which have one outcome. Whether it's a lack of appetite or emotional eating, stress influences our relationship with food. Some people feel they can't eat when stressed, this then causes a deficit in nutrition later down the line and eventually those people will go racing for the most energy dense foods (binging), some people crave the energy dense foods straight away (emotional eating). The issue here, is that sooner or later we are all craving the energy dense foods in order to prepare us for a fight or flight situation, the stress or anxiety is real, but the fighting and the flighting very rarely happens, and so the cycle begins again.

Our constant alert is tricking our brains into asking for food our body doesn't necessarily require, we are not working from zen tummy we are in full on panic survival mode. Our inner chimp is running loose thinking it is being chased by a tiger. There is no tiger, the chimp just can't differentiate between true external threat and an internal feeling of pain and self rejection. From an energetic perspective, this perceived threat felt at soul level, creates a craving for protection. We unconsciously feel the need for a barrier between us and the world, a need to try and control our surroundings. I see now how my body dysmorphia, my rejection of my physical body, caused me to be living in a constant fight or flight mode, what followed was chronic fatigue, a feeling that the world was not a safe place and a need to control my environment. It is my belief that controlling my food intake was me trying to take control of something in my life, trying to make life more predictable and within my power, because even though the enemy was in my own head, I perceived the threat as everywhere.

There are many existing ways we can de-stress our everyday lives; we can declutter our homes and create a sanctuary, we can sit for ten minutes of meditation, we can take walks in nature and take time for hobbies which bring us a sense of happiness. All valid and wonderful ways to reduce stress. But the issue with this is it doesn't necessarily remove our inner abusive voice, it just gives it some space in which to shout a little louder. I have lost count of the number of times, that I was sitting in meditation or holding a pose in yoga, worried that my tummy was sticking out or that others in the room thought I looked ridiculous. And so even when aiming to de-stress our lives, we can have an inner stress, a diatribe of self talk commentating on our appearance, our ability, our worth. The remedy for me was understanding why the negative self talk existed and treating the cause. Otherwise it's like complaining of monsters under the bed, scaring us at night and deciding that chopping the legs off the bed is the solution. The monsters usually just move to the wardrobe, or under the stairs.

Peace started for me, when I decided to have a conversation with the monsters and understand why they were there in the first place. Then we can move to a place where these critical thoughts are sidelined, moved aside or even made redundant. I believe the key is to reduce the perceived threat we have allowed to rage inside our minds and bodies. The monster inside our heads running around keeping us permanently engaged in fight or flight mode. The monster in our heads is the belief that we are not perfect, not worthy of being accepted into the sanctuary of a herd, the safety of community.

The solution from an external perspective is to create and nurture communities which are safe, supportive and operate on compassion, not competition and comparison. This not only reduces our perceived threat from outside, it creates a safe herd for us to belong to which increases our feeling of safety and reduces our day to day fight or flight response. I believe these communities are created with people who already have worked to lessen the threat within themselves, have broken away from the addiction cycle or at least have an awareness that their perceived threat comes from not feeling safe in ones own skin. The internal perspective is that by following the steps in this book, by reducing and finally removing the negative self talk, by being in harmony with your own body and with food, a peace will take it's place. This does not mean that I now dance around in a state of bliss every day, but through therapy, the steps in this book and diligent self care, I know that whatever life throws at me, I've got my own back, my mind and body are a compassionate team working together.

You Dear Soul, have chosen to read this book, and knowing that everything is divine timing, this must mean that you are on a journey of self worth and self acceptance, you are doing the work to live with compassion for self. From there you are perfectly placed to consciously create safe communities which will provide space for others to move from pain and fear, to compassion and understanding. How that takes shape for you is your divine purpose and your path, I know you are capable beyond your wildest dreams. And with a foundation of self care, your capacity for creating, is vast. This book and any creative projects I birth, are born of the time and headspace created when I healed my constant fear of rejection, my fear of not being good enough, of not being loveable, of not being worthy.

Dear Body

It is time we all stopped being ever ready to fight the lion or run from the tiger, it is time to thank the monsters and chimps for their service and to send them on their way. It is time to find sanctuary in our own bodies and it is most definitely time we used that place of peace within ourselves, to serve others in creating communities of compassion, cooperation and wellbeing. Your body is the temple from which you are able to hold your energy and to shine it on the world around you.

Chapter Twenty.

A Letter From Me To You.

Dear beautiful, unique, incredible soul,

Be gentle with yourself. Do not feel that failure means you are less than, you are simply on a journey, there is no wrong or right.

If you find you have become fearful, forgive yourself and choose again.

Stop and smile, catch the negative thoughts and smile lovingly at your inner child as you choose a more compassionate and loving transcript for your life. The miraculous body you have been given to navigate your human experience on this earth, is your partner for this journey.

Your body is not your enemy, we know how destructive it is to wage war and so we must choose to make peace with ourselves, we must choose to acknowledge that what makes us so lovable is our freedom from trying to be perfect.

What makes us so interesting is the capacity and time we have to explore and recount our passions and the time and capacity we have to listen to others.

What makes us extraordinary is we are meant to have had this struggle, we are meant to have not understood how to live with our body, we are meant to have had to learn how to nourish and care for it, how to learn to fuel ourselves with food and we are meant to have had to learn how to understand and choose our food, we are meant to learn how to be a human.

Always remember, you are pure potential, you are pure joy, you are compassion and you can express this with and through your human form. When your body is your cherished friend, you can express love to the wider

A Letter From Me To You

world in a way which can promote healing and change lives for the better.

You are the alchemist of your own biochemistry. You are not your body, you are not your mind, you are the awareness of body and mind, you are the light.

Your body is not a prison, it is a prism of light.

When you journey with your body as your friend, life takes on a feeling of freedom.

I hope this book has helped you on your journey of releasing your psyche from self rejection, and shown the power, the joy and the peace which comes from the mind accepting and loving the body which it inhabits. I hope you know the importance for your own wellbeing, the wellbeing of your loved ones and the wellbeing of the wider world, that you are a compassionate parent to yourself.

You are worthy, you are miraculous, you are loved, every bit of you.

With love always and for every-body,
Karen x

Appendices

Appendix A: Evidence of effect of thoughts on living things.

Dr Masaru Emoto, *The hidden messages in water*
Ernest Holmes & Willis Kinnear, *Thoughts are things*
Esther & Jerry Hicks, *Law of attraction*
Rhonda Byrne, *The secret*
Louise Hay, *You can heal your body*

Appendix B: Further reading

Brené Brown, *Daring greatly*
    The gifts of imperfection
Russell Brand, *Recovery*
Prof. Steve Peters, *The chimp paradox*
Colin Tipping, *Radical forgiveness*
Mel Robbins, *The high five habit*

Appendix C: Recommended reading for body health
Giulia Enders, *Gut*
Dr Bruce H. Lipton, *The biology of belief*
York food testing (**www.yorktest.com**)

Appendix D: Resources

The NHS website has a list of support and contact numbers
https://www.nhs.uk/live-well/healthy-body/getting-help-for-domestic-violence/

https://uksaysnomore.org/safespaces/
If you live outside the UK these resources may not be applicable, however the following link will advise how to cover your tracks should you want to search the internet for help in your area.

https://www.womensaid.org.uk/cover-your-tracks-online/

Printed in Great Britain
by Amazon